Human Rights in Focus: Illegal Immigrants

David M. Haugen

ReferencePoint Press®

San Diego, CA

About the Author

David M. Haugen is a film and English instructor at Ohio University. He also writes and edits books for publishers of educational reference materials.

© 2018 ReferencePoint Press, Inc.
Printed in the United States

For more information, contact:
ReferencePoint Press, Inc.
PO Box 27779
San Diego, CA 92198
www.ReferencePointPress.com

ALL RIGHTS RESERVED.
No part of this work covered by the copyright hereon may be reproduced or used in any form or by any means—graphic, electronic, or mechanical, including photocopying, recording, taping, web distribution, or information storage retrieval systems—without the written permission of the publisher.

Picture Credits

Cover: iStockphoto/Vichinterland
6: iStockphoto.com/vichinterlang
9: iStockphoto.com/lawcain
13: Justin Lane/EPA/Newscom
17: iStockphoto.com/vichinterlang
22: Brian Cahn/Zuma Press/Newscom
25: Roy Dabner/EPA/Newscom
28: Associated Press
34: Nic Bothma/EPA/Newscom
36: Scott McKiernan/Zuma Press/Newscom
41: Mayra Beltran/Rapport Press/Newscom
46: Martin H. Simon/UPI/Newscom
50: Associated Press
53: Mike Palazzotto/European Press Agency/ Newscom
58: Associated Press
61: Associated Press
65: CBP/Zuma Press/Newscom

LIBRARY OF CONGRESS CATALOGING-IN-PUBLICATION DATA

Name: Haugen, David M., 1969– author.
Title: Human Rights in Focus: Illegal Immigrants/by David M. Haugen.
Description: San Diego, CA: ReferencePoint Press, Inc., 2018. | Series: Human rights in focus | Includes bibliographical references and index. | Audience: Grade 9 to 12.
Identifiers: LCCN 2016045956 (print) | LCCN 2017005615 (ebook) | ISBN 9781682822296 (hardback) | ISBN 9781682822302 (eBook)
Subjects: LCSH: Illegal aliens—United States—Juvenile literature. | Illegal aliens—Government policy—United States—Juvenile literature. | Human rights—United States—Juvenile literature.
Classification: LCC JV6483 .H363 2018 (print) | LCC JV6483 (ebook) | DDC 364.1/37—dc23
LC record available at https://lccn.loc.gov/2016045956

Contents

Introduction

Between Sovereign Rights and Human Rights

Today most people take it for granted that all nations have a sovereign right to regulate the number of people who cross their borders. In the United States a body of immigration laws and policies dictate, for example, how many foreigners are allowed into the country and how many can take up legal residency. Likewise, statutes exist to define when foreigners have overstayed visitation privileges or when immigrants have crossed the nation's borders illegally. Together, these measures are what politicians and experts refer to when they speak about limiting, expanding, or otherwise reforming immigration.

Immigration laws are designed to manage immigrant populations, reassert a nation's boundaries, and help define what it means to be a citizen of a given country. Like all laws, they are intended to be carried out humanely and without discrimination. In the United States some of these policies grant specific protections to illegal immigrants that reflect the nation's concern for civil rights. However, some observers argue that these protections are not always enough to guarantee the welfare of immigrants who are arrested and deported. Others believe that the stated protections allow the government to ignore other human rights that might not be explicitly safeguarded in the laws.

Examining the Treatment of Illegal Immigrants

In a country where an estimated 11 million illegal immigrants have taken root and thousands more cross national borders each day, arrests, detentions, and deportations are commonplace. While many Americans believe that these are the consequences of unjust entry, few imagine that authorities might carry out their duties harshly or without respect for the welfare of those apprehended. According to some detainees, however, US Customs and Border Protection (CBP) agents and other law enforcement officers are not always evenhanded in their treatment of illegals. "I was just walking along when Border Patrol caught me," one twenty-one-year-old Mexican woman said. "They treated me really badly. They put me in a hielera."[1] *Hielera* is the Spanish word for "cooler," the nickname given to the heavily air-conditioned holding cells where captured illegals often wait for hours to be processed. "But some migrants are in Border Patrol cells for several days, without so much as a mat to lie on," Amy Bracken of Public Radio International reports. "Already, the holding cells are an unhappy crossroads between a difficult journey and a wildly uncertain future. And the discomfort of the place, some charge, is tantamount to abuse."[2]

Human rights advocates and organizations contend that existing international human rights treaties should ideally extend basic rights to all people at all times, even when these rights are not spelled out in the immigration laws (or any other policies or mandates) of a specific nation such as the United States. Opponents argue that international treaties do not supersede the Constitution. They point out that the US government's position has always been that international law is not binding for cases in which domestic law exists. Thus the government always adds provisions that state this view when negotiating international rights treaties. In terms of immigration, then, domestic laws are seen as taking priority over international agreements. Furthermore, government representatives try to assure critics that immigration authorities follow domestic regulations and do not abuse detainees in their care. CBP spokesperson Enrique Mendiola asserts that his agents rescue and save the lives of many illegal immigrants who are journeying through harsh terrain or hidden inside stiflingly hot vehicles to cross the southern border. "I would challenge anybody to compare the conditions that they may see when they come into our custody versus the conditions they were in when we found them in the brush, or in that 18-wheeler that was locked from the outside,"[3] Mendiola says.

> "Some migrants are in Border Patrol cells for several days, without so much as a mat to lie on."[2]
>
> —Amy Bracken, Public Radio International reporter

Some of the thousands of people who cross US borders every day do so illegally, leading to detentions and arrests. Here, a Border Patrol agent collects information from a family caught illegally entering the country in Texas.

An Ongoing Debate

Despite such assurances, human rights groups maintain that rights violations occur and that the government is bound to protect all people within the nation's borders whether they have entered legally or not. Even if such violations happen routinely, debate persists about how to resolve them. Some critics say that the government should not be compelled to look to international agreements to deal with internal immigration matters. Others are quick to remind rights advocates that illegal immigrants are themselves violating the law of the land and that the government already provides many amenities and services to these individuals during their detention. In a June 2014 editorial, Kristin Tate of the Breitbart News website used the feeding, housing, and even education of illegal immigrants at government expense to argue that undocumented individuals in detention facilities are treated better than America's homeless population. However, recent national polls indicate that the majority of Americans today have more tolerant views about illegal immigrants than past generations of Americans. As the treatment of undocumented detainees gains wider public attention, more citizens may begin to question US policies and practices.

Chapter 1

Deciding What Rights Apply to Undocumented Immigrants

For the United States, illegal immigration is a problem with many dimensions. Policy makers concerned with the issue tend to place emphasis on one or more of its controversial aspects. For some, the problem is that the federal government is not doing enough to stop the mostly Hispanic immigrants sneaking across the border between the United States and Mexico. For others, a greater concern is the deporting of millions of illegal immigrants who live and work in US communities. Still others worry about the possibility of terrorist infiltration among the thousands of foreigners who gain illegal access to the country each day.

Much of the illegal immigration debate highlights fears about America's vulnerability and about the supposed degradation of American values and the economy. A March 2016 Pew Research Center poll reported that 33 percent of Americans believe illegal immigrants are a burden on the country because they take jobs, housing, and health care away from citizens. A December 2015 survey by Quinnipiac University noted that 27 percent of Americans supported banning people of Muslim faith from entering the United States. Such fears drive immigration debates, and they reveal a clear concern for protecting the rights of citizens. However, other interested parties believe that illegal immigration discussions and policies should equally take into consideration the rights of the immigrants. Human rights activists, for example, insist that harsh immigration policies typically disregard the plight of immigrants and the inhumane treatment they suffer both on their journey to America and once they arrive. They contend that the sovereignty of the nation must be balanced against its commitment to the respect for human life and the dignity of all people. These activists also believe that this commitment demonstrates how America is progressing as a global citizen. To chart that progress, though, it is worthwhile to examine the nation's past bouts with immigration issues; as Charles Hirschman, a sociology professor at the University of Washington, states, "The current debates and hostility surrounding immigrants echo throughout American history."[4]

A Brief History of US Immigration Laws

While many American immigration laws and policies have existed for some time, they were not established during the country's infancy. After all, the colonies that would become the United States were founded by immigrants coming from England, Holland, Germany, and Scandinavia—all who arrived largely without fear of being turned away from its shores. Typically, a criminal record was the only grounds for rejection of a European immigrant by an established colony. Non-Europeans also quickly began arriving on American shores, though not always by their own will. Beginning in the 1600s, slaves were brought from Africa without any thought of immigration or resettlement issues. Even after the American colonies formed a nation in the eighteenth century, their collective law—the US Constitution—failed to make explicit reference to immigration in any of the powers afforded to the federal government.

The first congressional attempt to limit immigration did not occur until 1875, when the Page Act addressed the problems of prostitution and forced labor among Chinese immigrants in the newly settled West. The act empowered the US embassy in Hong Kong to keep "undesirable" women and other "lowly" individuals (who were thought to carry infectious diseases) from immigrating to the United States. Later, between World War I and World War II, the Emergency Quota Act of 1921 set limits on the number of immigrants—chiefly from Europe—allowed to enter the United States. The immigration of professional-class Europeans was not restricted. Instead, the law was aimed at keeping poor southern and eastern Europeans from fleeing political and ethnic instability in their homelands and bringing their vices and anarchist ideologies to America while offering no useful skills in return. Then in 1930, during the onset of the Great Depression, the federal gov-

The US Constitution, intended to govern a nation made up largely of people from other lands, makes no explicit reference to immigration in any of the powers assigned to the federal government.

ernment began denying visas to Mexican migrant workers and expelling over 1 million already in the country in hopes of opening up job opportunities to native workers.

Turning away and actively deporting immigrants became routine in the early to mid-twentieth century. For example, Italian immigrants were denied entry because of concerns over possible Mafia affiliations in the 1920s and 1930s. By the 1950s, however, it was Mexican laborers who would be most identified with

The Universal Declaration of Human Rights

Although human rights advocates draw from many of the thirty articles within the Universal Declaration of Human Rights in defending undocumented immigrants from persecution, the first seven articles define the dignity of the individual and his or her integrity before the law.

Article 1: All human beings are born free and equal in dignity and rights. They are endowed with reason and conscience and should act towards one another in a spirit of brotherhood.

Article 2: Everyone is entitled to all the rights and freedoms set forth in this Declaration, without distinction of any kind, such as race, colour, sex, language, religion, political or other opinion, national or social origin, property, birth or other status. Furthermore, no distinction shall be made on the basis of the political, jurisdictional or international status of the country or territory to which a person belongs. . . .

Article 3: Everyone has the right to life, liberty and security of person.

Article 4: No one shall be held in slavery or servitude; slavery and the slave trade shall be prohibited in all their forms.

Article 5: No one shall be subjected to torture or to cruel, inhuman or degrading treatment or punishment.

Article 6: Everyone has the right to recognition everywhere as a person before the law.

Article 7: All are equal before the law and are entitled without any discrimination to equal protection of the law. All are entitled to equal protection against any discrimination in violation of this Declaration and against any incitement to such discrimination.

United Nations General Assembly, Universal Declaration of Human Rights, December 10, 1948. www.un.org.

undocumented immigration and deportation efforts in the United States. The bracero program, begun in 1942 when most young, white men were fighting overseas, allowed some Mexican farm laborers to take up temporary residency in the United States to work on large agricultural plantations in Texas, California, and other parts of the Southwest. While the braceros applied for these jobs through legal channels, many other hopeful Mexican workers came across the border illegally to fill the growing need for fieldworkers.

By 1954, several years after World War II had ended, President Dwight Eisenhower instructed border authorities to round up these illegals and return them to Mexico. Attorney General Herbert Brownell claimed that because of the influx of illegal immigrants, the country "was faced with a breakdown in law enforcement on a very large scale." He added, "When I say large scale, I mean hundreds of thousands were coming in from Mexico [every year] without restraint."[5] Operation Wetback—as the roundup was called—caught more than 1 million illegal immigrants in its first year, sending the majority deep into Mexican territory (with the cooperation of the Mexican government) to discourage their return. The program ended in 1962, but the fears that Brownell expressed—along with complaints that illegal immigration was hurting the job opportunities of native-born Americans—remained talking points of the illegal immigration debate.

The government and the courts have upheld immigration laws through much of the nation's modern history. Although quotas were dropped, America has continually sought to limit immigration by giving preferential treatment to only those foreigners who apply for citizenship through proper channels. Concern over too many Mexican immigrants arriving illegally still occupies the heart of discussions about unregulated or unlimited immigration. The reason Mexican immigrants have become the face of illegal immigration in the United States has much to do with America's porous southern border, but as author Francisco Balderrama points out, it is also because Mexican immigrants "are the most recent immigrant group to come to the United States in the early 20th century."[6]

The Legal Rights Afforded to Illegal Immigrants

While America has built up a history of laws to deal with immigration, some rights organizations are troubled with how these laws are applied and what motivates the nation to enforce them sometimes inhumanely. These organizations wish to see immigrants treated with respect, and they look for protections that might apply to illegal immigrants even as laws compel their arrest and deportation. For example, observers often argue that, even though the Constitution does not address immigrants specifically, all people within the nation's borders are protected by the Bill of Rights. Therefore, undocumented immigrants are afforded the right to a speedy and public trial, the right to legal representation, and the assurance of due process. All of these protections definitely apply if illegal immigrants are prosecuted for criminal wrongdoing. However, as the online magazine *Slate* explains, this is rarely the case, because "immigration proceedings are matters of administrative law, not criminal law."[7] On the one hand, an illegal immigrant who commits a crime might be arrested, tried in the courts, and thrown in jail. On the other hand, an illegal immigrant who is simply caught in hiding is not imprisoned for a crime but instead deported.

This is not to suggest that illegal immigrants have no protections. Indeed, the Fourteenth Amendment guarantees that "no state shall . . . deprive any person of life, liberty or property, without due process of law; nor deny to any person within its jurisdiction the equal protection of the laws." Illegal immigrants who are caught have the right to defend themselves against deportation, and they possess the right to a hearing before an immigration judge. They also have the right to be represented by legal counsel, although unlike criminal defendants, an undocumented individual does not have the right to have a lawyer appointed and paid for by the government.

Even if not the subject of capture, illegal immigrants have other rights that they and others might not know about. For instance, illegal immigrants who are working in the United States have a right to be paid at least at the level of state-determined minimum wage. Undocumented workers also have the right to work in safe conditions and cannot be discriminated against based on race, ethnicity, or nationality. In fact, undocumented workers have the right to file lawsuits against employers for violating these protections. Of course, many illegal immigrants

"Because immigration is considered a matter of national security and foreign policy, the Supreme Court has long held that immigration law is largely immune from judicial review. Congress can make rules for immigrants that would be unacceptable if applied to citizens."[8]

—*Slate*, an Internet news magazine

After the 2010 attempted terrorist attack in New York City's Times Square (pictured), US attorney general Eric Holder recommended that authorities be allowed to question terrorist suspects without informing them of their right to remain silent.

do not utilize these rights, because they fear that they will suffer job loss or even deportation for making themselves heard.

A Climate of Fear

It is Congress and not the court system that guarantees the rights of illegal immigrants, and it is Congress that can alter them, abridge them, or take them away. "Congress has nearly full authority to regulate immigration without interference from the courts," *Slate* notes. "Because immigration is considered a matter of national security and foreign policy, the Supreme Court has long held that immigration law is largely immune from judicial review. Congress can make rules for immigrants that would be unacceptable if applied to citizens."[8] Some critics are suspicious of Congress's power to define the rights granted to undocumented immigrants. They worry that legislators may act impulsively or be swayed by sensationalized events in ways that would infringe on basic human rights. For example, in the wake of the failed 2010 terrorist bombing in New York City's Times Square, Attorney General Eric Holder told a morning news program that Congress should consider legislation to permit authorities to question terrorism suspects without first informing

The Constitution Versus International Law

Most critics who argue that US law supersedes international law cite the supremacy clause of the Constitution, which states: "This Constitution, and the Laws of the United States which shall be made in pursuance thereof; and all treaties made, or which shall be made, under the authority of the United States, shall be the supreme law of the land." Writer Greg Stuessel, for example, argues, "Treaties must be made: 'in pursuance' of the Constitution's delegated powers as well. To do otherwise is a serious usurpation of the very nature of our Constitutional Republic. To allow foreign law to trump the Supreme Law of the Land leaves the people of this nation in a precarious situation at best with their liberties."

On the other hand, those who promote the power of international law maintain that governments agree to be bound by such laws and do so to make the global community more just. Law professor Douglass Cassel adds:

> Because international human rights treaties are adopted by governments, usually after prolonged and contested negotiations and followed in many countries by lengthy processes of ratification, they confer legitimacy on claims of rights, especially when those claims are asserted (as they usually are) against governments. Human rights groups can (and regularly do) say to governments, "It is not *we* who say that torture is illegal and must be investigated and punished; it is *you* who so declare, as parties to the Convention Against Torture."

The debate over the application of human rights law to illegal immigration issues highlights this conflict of loyalties.

Greg Stuessel, "Do Treaties Trump the Constitution?," *Before It's News*, June 22, 2013. www.beforeitsnews.com.

Douglass Cassel, "Does International Human Rights Law Make a Difference?," *Scholarly Works*, Notre Dame Law School, 2001. http://scholarship.law.nd.edu.

them of their right to remain silent. This is a safeguard afforded to all suspects because of the Fifth Amendment's protection against self-incrimination. No such law was passed, but the comment suggested that the nation's most powerful legal counsel was more concerned about public safety than individual rights. "The great fear is that when the government has the power to strip some people of basic rights, it cannot be easily limited,"[9] states Erwin Chemerinsky, dean of the University of California–Irvine School of Law.

Many people are fearful that illegal immigration poses a danger to the United States. In a 2012 discussion about cracking down on undocumented immigrants in the Southwest, Representative Phil Roe of Tennessee stated, "Illegal immigration is a serious threat to our national security, one that is very expensive and a burden to hardworking taxpayers."[10] Roe's assertion was not specifically targeting threats from the numerous Hispanic workers that have crossed the southern border but rather the fact that unmonitored borders allow others—such as criminals and terrorists—to easily infiltrate the nation.

Regardless of whether illegal immigration facilitates terrorism, many Americans believe illegal immigrants are responsible for a host of criminal activities, especially along the southern border. Peter B. Gemma, National Executive Committee member of the Constitution Party, a group promoting conservative Christian values, claims that evidence exists to link illegal immigrants with increased rates of car theft, drunken driving, and drug-related charges in the border regions. Gemma adds:

> The overall perspective of the criminal behavior of illegal aliens is grim. In a 2007 Government Accountability Office study of 55,322 illegal aliens, analysts discovered that they were arrested at least a total of 459,614 times, averaging about eight arrests per illegal alien: 70 percent had between two and 10 arrests, and 26 percent (about 15,000) had 11 or more arrests. Drug or immigration offenses accounted for 45 percent of all offenses, and approximately 12 percent (over 6,600 illegal aliens) were arrested for violent offenses such as murder, robbery, assault, and sex-related crimes.[11]

These assessments as well as reports that Mexican drug cartels are bringing violence and bloodshed to border communities inflame the public's fears of border crossers. President Donald Trump broadcast these fears in the public forum and made them a platform for his presidential campaign when he announced his candidacy in June 2015. "When Mexico sends its people, they're not sending their best," Trump declared. "They're bringing drugs. They're bringing crime. They're rapists." Then, he added, "And some, I assume, are good people."[12]

Advocating Human Rights Law

Because such fears are pervasive in the debates about illegal immigration, those who are concerned about the treatment and welfare of illegal immigrants contend that the government should do more to guarantee and protect the rights of immigrants. Sociology and American studies professor Tanya Golash-Boza asserts that "the United States has a strong tradition of civil and political rights, yet, unlike most other nations, it does not give much weight to the social, economic, or cultural rights that are central to the human rights tradition."[13] The rights she refers to are spelled out in the American Declaration of the Rights and Duties of Man, an international document signed by the United States in 1948, as well as the United Nations (UN) Universal Declaration of Human Rights also adopted that year. Within these documents are guarantees, for example, that all people possess a right to work, a right to participate in cultural activities that enrich intellect and make individuals feel part of a community, and a right to establish a family and protect it from disruption or harm.

> "The United States has a strong tradition of civil and political rights, yet, unlike most other nations, it does not give much weight to the social, economic, or cultural rights that are central to the human rights tradition."[13]
>
> —Tanya Golash-Boza, sociology and American studies professor at the University of California–Merced

To Golash-Boza and others who advocate the broader application of human rights to illegal immigrants, the nation has an ethical responsibility to treat undocumented individuals with dignity. This includes upholding human rights during routine identification checks, roundups, detentions, and deportations. She believes that an emphasis on these internationally agreed-upon norms would put America in line with other countries that have incorporated human rights concerns into their national immigration laws. "All people, regardless of their country of birth, deserve to be treated with dignity and respect," Golash-Boza writes. "U.S. immigration laws fall short of the realization of the human rights of immigrants and their family members in countless ways." In an attempt to enumerate, she claims that current policy "leads to at least five key rights violations: 1) The right to form a family; 2) the right to due process; 3) the right to freedom from discrimination; 4) the right to freedom from arbitrary detention; and 5) the right to not experience cruel or unusual punishment."[14]

The UN and other international groups have warned the United States and other nations in the recent past about policies that seem to violate ratified international human rights accords. One such incident took place in 2010, when Arizona implemented a law that gave police the power to arrest or otherwise detain individuals based on "reasonable suspicion" that they are in the country illegally. In response, the Global Migration Group—a combination of UN agencies, the World Bank, and the International Organization for Migration—issued a statement to clarify its expectations of the US government in regard to the potential for racial profiling and abuse. Navi Pillay, the UN High Commissioner for Human Rights, said the public statement served as "a reminder that while states are entitled to regulate movement across their borders they must do so in accordance with their obligations under international law including international human rights law."[15]

A Border Patrol agent collects the personal belongings of a woman being detained in Texas for entering the country illegally. Advocates say that the United States has an ethical obligation to treat such individuals with dignity and protect their human rights.

Defending Sovereignty

Not everyone agrees, though, that international law should rule domestic affairs. Jack Goldsmith, a Harvard law professor, argues that international treaties that demand governments bend to global pressures only encourage resentment. That is, governments and their people may feel that international lawmaking that tries to legislate what goes on within a nation's borders undercuts sovereign control. In addition, the call for nations to adhere strictly to such international laws might imply that those nations are either too weak-willed or too dictatorial to govern themselves properly. Some critics also fear that this kind of blind adherence may overlook specific cultural values or historical circumstances that matter to the population affected by these laws. Goldsmith writes, "When the human rights community demands that the United States make international human rights treaties a part of domestic law in a way that circumvents political control, it evinces an intolerance for a pluralism of values and conditions, and a disrespect for local democratic processes."[16]

> "When the human rights community demands that the United States make international human rights treaties a part of domestic law in a way that circumvents political control, it evinces an intolerance for a pluralism of values and conditions, and a disrespect for local democratic processes."[16]
>
> —Jack Goldsmith, law professor at Harvard University

Jeremy Rabkin, a law professor at George Mason University and the author of *Why Sovereignty Matters*, looks at the roots of this problem. He maintains that civil liberties organizations within the United States who clamor for more attention to human rights in US law believe the international community is acting with the same vigor and compassion as the US Supreme Court during the era of civil rights reform. Rabkin writes:

> Yet judicial activism was effective in the United States—to the extent that it was—because most Americans, including most government officials, had great respect for their own Constitution and great reserves of loyalty to Court rulings, even if they did not agree with them. It is hard to see how we teach respect for constitutional democracy by

establishing a system of free-floating international appeals, hovering above every actual constitutional state.[17]

To Rabkin and others, the danger of this belief is that government constitutions and national elections become a façade—no longer reflecting the will of the governed.

An Uncertain Future

Whether US immigration policy will be shaped by human rights concerns is a matter of debate. However, human rights advocates continue to press the government to show a stronger commitment to the protection of these rights in the treatment of undocumented immigrants in America. To date, the government has asserted its sovereignty in domestic affairs—such as immigration—by ensuring that international agreements do not take precedence over national law. The United States has often taken a leading role in pointing out other nations' human rights abuses. However, the US government may find itself struggling to appear as a champion of international law if it continues to pick and choose which parts of international agreements it will abide by and which parts it will ignore.

Chapter 2

Harassment and Exploitation

Focus Questions

1. What kind of restrictions or penalties, if any, do you think illegal immigrants should be subject to while living in the United States, and why?
2. Do you think it is appropriate for police officers to stop people of a certain physical appearance and inquire about their immigration status? Why or why not?
3. Should human rights considerations trump or be made part of US immigration law? Explain why or why not.

In June 2011 Alabama governor Robert Bentley signed the Beason-Hammon Alabama Taxpayer and Citizen Protection Act (HB 56) into law. At over seventy pages in length, the legislation was extensive yet focused on one specific group of people—undocumented immigrants. The purpose of the bill was to deny illegal immigrants the use of any state services, but one of its sponsors, State Representative Micky Hammon, asserted the law "attacks every aspect of an illegal alien's life," pressuring them into "self-deportation."[18] Within its regulations, the Beason-Hammon Act threatened to fine or jail undocumented workers who applied for jobs or any noncitizen who could not produce a valid visa or verify legal resident status. Schools and universities were charged with verifying such status before enrolling students. Businesses and landlords were prohibited from entering into contracts with undocumented persons, and these entities could be fined or have their licenses revoked if found in violation of this law. Finally, the Alabama Department of Homeland Security was authorized to create its own police force to monitor illegals and process verifications from businesses and other state entities. This enforcement unit as well as regular state police were also granted the right to detain individuals based on reasonable suspicion of undocumented status, and any person arrested for a crime that required bail had to submit to legal status verification.

Civil liberties and human rights organizations were quick to speak out against the law and threaten suits against the state. The American Civil Liberties Union (ACLU) said the act would "deter children from going to school, deny people public benefits to which they are lawfully entitled, and interfere with their ability to rent housing, earn a living, and enter into contracts."[19] Judicial review from within the Alabama courts and the circuit court system blocked portions of the bill—including the verification of schoolchildren's legal status—while the rest went through litigation. Even the US Department of Justice joined a coalition of civil rights groups to bring suit against the state, and in 2013 many of its provisions were permanently blocked after the state settled with the assembled plaintiffs. For example, immigrants no longer had to carry identification papers, citizens could not be criminalized for entering into contracts with undocumented persons for housing or business purposes, undocumented workers could seek employment and be paid for their labor, and law enforcement could not detain individuals merely for suspicion of illegal status.

Both sides in the two-year legal struggle claimed victory. Hammon stated that the heart of the law was still enforceable. By this he meant that colleges and universities must still check immigration status of students, all Alabama-based businesses must use the federal E-Verify system to check an employee's eligibility to work, and police officers could check the legal status of anyone they arrested, even if they could no longer arrest people simply for suspicion of being undocumented. The ACLU, the Southern Poverty Law Center (SPLC), and others reveled in the defeat of what they believed to be the most severe and harmful measures, but they cautioned that vigilance was still needed to end discrimination against illegal immigrants. Writing for the American Immigration Council in 2013, Amanda Peterson Beadle commented

People gather in Birmingham, Alabama, in November 2011 to protest the anti-immigration law HB 56, which was intended to deny undocumented immigrants the use of any state services.

on the broader impact of the settlement. "The agreement that permanently blocks some of the worst portions of HB 56 as well as the lasting scars it caused," she asserted, "should be a warning to other states that may consider similarly damaging laws."[20]

Far-Reaching State Laws

The Alabama law was not the first of its kind, nor is the zeal to pursue illegals through federal statutes and state laws uncommon. In November 2013 Muzaffar Chishti and Faye Hipsman of the Migration Policy Institute wrote, "While states have historically sought and had a role in policies affecting noncitizens, their engagement in enforcement of federal immigration laws began in earnest in the mid-1990s and gained speed over the past three years as state legislators moved to enact omnibus laws designed to encourage unauthorized immigrants to leave or discourage them from settling." In 2010 Arizona became the first state to enact severe and controversial legislation (SB 1070) targeting illegals. "Alabama, Georgia, Indiana, South Carolina, and Utah—quickly followed Arizona's example in 2011, with the Alabama law considered the most far-reaching and stringent of these measures,"[21] Chishti and Hipsman say.

Showing its distaste for Alabama's law, Human Rights Watch insisted the legislation was "intended by its sponsors to make everyday life unlivable for unauthorized immigrants to the United States." The organization argued that the law deprived undocumented persons of international human rights protections in addition to basic constitutional safeguards. In Human Rights Watch's opinion, the legal actions of governments must not violate basic human or civil rights granted to everyone through national laws or international accords. "While every state in the United States has a population of people who entered the country illegally who may lawfully be subject to deportation," the organization contends, "no federal or state law may create a situation in which fundamental rights due all persons are infringed upon."[22]

Human Rights Watch and other watchdog groups maintain that these unfriendly laws violate several human rights agreed on by the United States and the international community. According to the ACLU, for example, the attempts by Arizona, Alabama, and other states to enact laws that empower police to detain individuals based on suspicion of undocumented status is a violation of the International Covenant on Civil and Political Rights (ICCPR) and the International Convention on the Elimination of All Forms of Racial Discrimination (ICERD). These treaties were ratified in 1966 and 1969, respectively. Both assert that all people should be free from discrimination either through exclusion or preference. The ICERD even calls on national governments to "amend, rescind or nullify any laws and regulations, which have the effect of creating or perpetuating racial discrimination."[23]

> "[Alabama's HB 25 immigration law is] intended by its sponsors to make everyday life unlivable for unauthorized immigrants to the United States."[22]
>
> —Human Rights Watch, an international organization that advocates for human rights

Racial Profiling

To rights-focused organizations like the ACLU, allowing police to stop individuals who look like they might be undocumented is a form of racial profiling because only a certain section of the population would be likely targets. Chief among these targeted races or ethnicities in Arizona and Alabama are people of Hispanic descent. When Arizona's SB 1070 law went into effect in 2010, Chris Good of the *Atlantic* noted, "Officers probably won't be stopping a lot of white people, since all illegal Mexican immigrants are, by definition, Mexican—meaning most of them will be Hispanic—thus almost all of the erroneous stops, the collateral damage of enforcing Arizona's new law, will be inflicted upon the Hispanic population."[24] Racial profiling is the type of discrimination that the US agreed should be opposed under constitutional guarantees and human rights conventions. During the 2005 meeting of the UN Commission on Human Rights, the ACLU pointed out that "under the ICCPR, the United States is not only to cease from engaging in racial profiling on a national level, but also to actively monitor the policing activities of law enforcement agencies at all levels in order to identify racial profiling and put an end to it."[25]

While the ACLU reminder was written in response to the racial profiling of African Americans by police departments, the organization has since called on the articles of the ICCPR in the fight against racial profiling of undocumented persons of Hispanic descent. In 2008 the ACLU issued a paper that examined the issue of motorists being pulled over for the "crime" of DWB—"driving while black or brown." In that paper, the ACLU noted that in Arizona, more people of color had been stopped, questioned, detained, and cited than white motorists. After the passage of the Arizona law, the state continued to be the focus of racial profiling concerns because of the enforcement efforts of Sheriff Joe Arpaio of Maricopa County. Arpaio had been accused for years of instructing his department to use race as a reason for pulling over motorists and conducting searches. Arpaio was summoned before a federal court in 2013 after an investigation of the Maricopa County Sheriff's Office. During the court hearing, the

> "Under the ICCPR, the United States is not only to cease from engaging in racial profiling on a national level, but also to actively monitor the policing activities of law enforcement agencies at all levels in order to identify racial profiling and put an end to it."[25]
>
> —The ACLU, a nonprofit organization that champions individual rights

judge stated that investigators had confirmed the department was using race as a factor in making traffic stops. Arpaio was ordered to stop the practice, but he was back before the same judge in July 2016 for violating that order. In October of that year, the US Department of Justice formally charged Arpaio with a misdemeanor for continuing to utilize racial profiling. If convicted, he could spend up to six months in jail, though he would not lose his office.

Racial profiling has created a climate of fear for illegal immigrants in some US communities. In talking to undocumented individuals and families in Alabama after the passage of the Beason-Hammon Act, Human Rights Watch found that most adapted to living "underground." The group's report acknowledged, "Nearly every unauthorized immigrant interviewed by Human Rights Watch reported curtailing everyday activities. To minimize the risk of being stopped by the police while driving, families reported

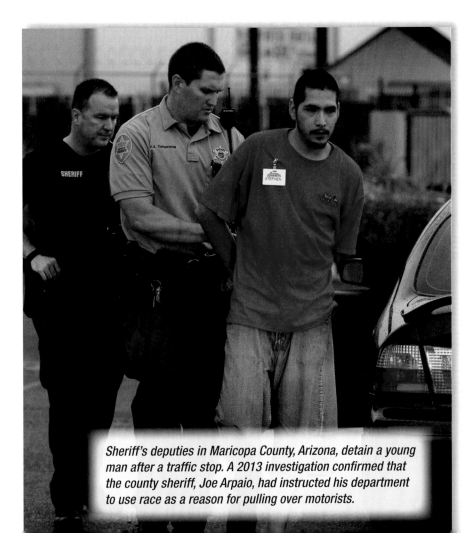

Sheriff's deputies in Maricopa County, Arizona, detain a young man after a traffic stop. A 2013 investigation confirmed that the county sheriff, Joe Arpaio, had instructed his department to use race as a reason for pulling over motorists.

staying home as much as possible, driving only to go to work or buy necessities."[26] Many illegals stated they stopped taking their children—who are often legal residents of the country by birth—to sports activities, church events, or other community functions because they did not want to drive more than necessary and risk being pulled over by police looking to stop individuals of a certain skin color. According to Human Rights Watch and others, such a climate of fear directly contradicts the safeguards of the American Declaration of the Rights and Duties of Man and the Universal Declaration of Human Rights, both of which proclaim the rights to leisure time and to the benefits of culture.

Harassment of Illegal Workers

Human rights organizations have long pointed out that communities, states, or nations that authorize law enforcement to selectively target undocumented persons are sending a message to the larger public that abusing or harassing illegal immigrants is tolerated. Human Rights Watch's interviews revealed cases of Alabamans slighting anyone of assumed Hispanic descent. Among those who offered testimony, "Suzanna Collerd, an organizer with Alabama Coalition for Immigrant Justice, reported she had spoken with a woman who was asked for her identification when she asked to look at some jewelry at a major discount department store, and another woman who could not get her warranty honored at a major electronics retailer without an Alabama driver's license." In other instances, the discrimination was more blatant: "Some people reported that even strangers at grocery stores have made abusive remarks, such as, 'Why are you still here? Don't you understand you have to leave?'"[27]

In such an environment of unfriendliness, illegal immigrants face other forms of discrimination—especially at the workplace or during job hunts. Some communities, for example, have tried to ban day laborers from congregating on streets or to make it illegal for contractors to hire these individuals. In several cases these bans have been deemed unconstitutional. In San Francisco in 2006, for instance, a federal judge ruled that disallowing day laborers—who are largely made up of undocumented Hispanic males—from asking for work was a violation of free speech rights. Other courts have come to different conclusions. A circuit court

Racial Profiling Can Be Justified in Dealing with Immigrant Communities

DumpDC is an editorial website that opposes expansive federal government powers and supports state secession. Russell D. Longcore, the editor in chief of DumpDC, explains why he believes Arizona's law that grants officers the power to stop individuals based on reasonable suspicion of undocumented status is just.

> The Arizona immigration law [SB 1070] does not abridge the privileges or immunities of citizens of the United States. It does not deprive any person of life, liberty or property without due process of law.
>
> What the immigration law does is acknowledge that the predominance of illegal immigrants in Arizona are Latinos, and as such, empowers law enforcement personnel to use their common sense to investigate whether any individual Latino human being can proffer verifiable identification and proof of US citizenship. Said another way—if we know that nearly every illegal immigrant in Arizona has Latino physical characteristics, it is not an "unreasonable search" to require that they produce identification and proof of citizenship.

Russell D. Longcore, "Arizona, Immigration and Racial Profiling: Liberal Panties Are in a Wad," DumpDC, May 7, 2010. www.dumpdc.wordpress.com.

ruled in 2010 that a law banning day laborers from congregating in and around Redondo Beach, California, did not infringe on the free speech of the workers because it regulates conduct and not any specific verbal message.

Laws that prohibit the hiring of undocumented workers do not deter many businesses from seeking out this labor force. Public Policy Institute of California researcher Arturo Gonzalez states:

> Ordinances don't do anything to erase the demand for day laborers. Our statewide study [of 2007] finds that about half the employers of all day laborers are private individuals, often residents of the same community where the laborer was hired. These employers continue to draw and bring day laborers back into the same cities that expelled them—to meet the same demand for gardeners, landscapers, handymen, etc. that existed before.[28]

Day laborers wait for work outside a home improvement store in Phoenix. Some communities have tried to ban these workers from assembling in this manner.

However, such ordinances coupled with other anti-immigrant policies and sentiment might prompt business owners to exploit and abuse undocumented laborers.

Feeling Powerless

In 2010 the SPLC studied the plight of undocumented women workers and found that many were exploited and even abused. "Because of their status, they fill the lowest-paying jobs in the country. They typically earn minimum wage or less, get no sick or vacation days, and receive no health insurance," the organization states. After conducting interviews with many women in the food industry (including agricultural laborers), the SPLC found that all felt disposable and had been cheated out of wages at one time or another. According to the SPLC:

> Many of those employed in farm work said they have been sickened by pesticides and toxic chemicals. Those working in meat and poultry processing said they labored long hours in bone-chilling temperatures with inadequate safety equipment. Many of the women reported being denied ac-

cess to bathrooms or barred from taking time off to tend to emergencies like sick children—even when they worked for huge corporate employers required by law to provide those benefits. Some faced illegal discrimination because of pregnancy.[29]

Most of these women feel powerless to stop such abuses, and according to the SPLC, poor treatment is not confined to the food industry. In a 2012 SPLC report on the impact of the Beason-Hammon Act, women workers in other jobs faced similar injustices. One undocumented woman told of being hired by a man to clear trees from a plot of land and remove moldy and infested furniture from a trailer. When the woman went to collect her wages from the man at his home, she was told that she had done a poor job. Even though all the work had been completed, the man refused to pay her, brandishing a gun to scare her away. She filed a complaint with police, but nothing came of it. She felt she had no recourse to resolve the issue fairly. "You can't fight with anyone if you aren't legal, and that's why he didn't pay us," the woman told the SPLC. "We haven't gone to the court because it's like we have no case because we're illegal. We're afraid to do it."[30]

In a 2012 report on migrant farmworkers, Human Rights Watch interviewed several illegal immigrant women who attested to being cheated on the job and sexually harassed or raped. "Farmworkers reported incidents of humiliating, debilitating harassment in the form of unwanted touching, pressure to engage in sexual relations, and verbal harassment," the report claimed. Human Rights Watch provided no statistics on the number of workers who have been sexually harassed, but the organization maintains that nearly every interviewee had been a victim or knew someone personally who had experienced harassment or rape. "Our research confirms what farmworker advocates across the country believe: sexual violence and sexual harassment experienced by farmworkers is common enough that some farmworker women see these abuses as an unavoidable condition of agricultural work."[31]

Hurting Every Worker

Exploitation of undocumented workers is not confined to women. Many of these workers—regardless of gender—have reported being cheated of wages, receiving low wages in comparison to legal workers, and experiencing other forms of exploitation. Twenty-six-year-old Antonio Vanegas, an illegal immigrant, found work in a restaurant in the Ronald Reagan Building in Washington, DC. The structure is ironically also the home of the CBP. Vanegas told the *Huffington Post* in 2013 that he was paid under the table and below the established minimum wage. When he took part in a strike organized by advocates of unionizing low-wage workers in government buildings, he spoke out about his substandard treatment. Then, when he showed up for work a few days later, he was met by US Department of Homeland Security (DHS) officers, who detained him and set him up with a deportation hearing. "This country is a country of laws," Vanegas said. "Regardless of my status, I should have some protections based on the labor laws that have been violated."[32] Instead, like many

Racial Profiling Is Not Justified in Dealing with Immigrant Communities

The Leadership Conference on Civil and Human Rights, a nonprofit coalition of human rights advocacy groups, contends that racial profiling under Arizona law has only created fear and tension between law enforcement and immigrant communities.

Local law enforcement authorities now profile entire communities as they assume duties of immigration enforcement. . . . Nowhere is there a clearer illustration of the abuses inherent in such community-wide policing actions than in Maricopa County, Arizona, where Sheriff Joe Arpaio has received national attention for his aggressive "Driving While Brown" profiling of Hispanic drivers, as well as his sweeps of Hispanic communities. In the most notorious of these neighborhood sweeps, Arpaio sent more than 100 deputies, a volunteer posse, and a helicopter into a community of approximately 6,000 Yaqui Indians and Hispanics outside Phoenix. For two days, this outsized police presence stopped residents on the street, chased them into their homes, and generally terrorized community members so completely that many will not come out of their homes if they see a sheriff's patrol car. By the time the operation had ended, a total of only nine undocumented immigrants had been arrested.

Leadership Conference on Civil and Human Rights, "Restoring a National Consensus: The Need to End Racial Profiling in America," March 2011. www.civilrights.org.

other undocumented workers, Vanegas was informed on by his boss, who did not want the headache of dealing with a troublesome employee. "When undocumented workers are trying to organize, they're threatened with deportation, and that keeps everyone's wages down," Kyle de Beausset, a senior member of the organizers, said. "We're hopeful this will help people realize that when folks are here in the country and unable to organize, it hurts everyone."[33]

Human rights advocates insist that the nation has a responsibility to guard all workers—and all individuals—against exploitation and harassment. "Both international law and US law recognize that all workers, including unauthorized immigrant workers, are entitled to the same workplace protections as US workers. These provisions exist to minimize employers' incentives to hire an easily exploitable workforce,"[34] Human Rights Watch claims. But these guarantees are not evenly enforced. In addition, human rights activists worry that states and federal authorities are focused on apprehending illegal immigrants and quickly channeling them through the deportation system. This could lead, they believe, to abuses of undocumented populations being ignored and their human rights largely disregarded.

"This country is a country of laws. Regardless of my status, I should have some protections based on the labor laws that have been violated."[32]

—Antonio Vanegas, an undocumented worker who lost his job after taking part in a strike

Chapter 3

Detention and Deportation

Focus Questions

1. How long do you think is appropriate for immigration enforcement agencies to detain illegal immigrants awaiting removal or a hearing? What evidence can you supply to justify your decision?
2. What services do you think all detained illegal immigrants should have access to, and why? Are there any services they should not have access to, and why?
3. Do you believe that human rights organizations are trying to prevent the United States from enforcing its own immigration laws? Why or why not?

In 2000 thirteen-year-old David Thomas arrived in the United States with his parents and siblings. He and his family were fleeing civil war in their home country of Liberia. Like many other Liberians at that time, the Thomases were granted resettlement privileges as refugees in the United States. David and his family adjusted to American life quickly; David enrolled in school, and over the next few years he began playing football, eventually earning an athletic scholarship to college. By age twenty-one he was attending California State University, Sacramento, and raising two children with his girlfriend. A domestic spat, however, landed David in jail on battery charges. He served his thirty days and was released, but the incident put him on the radar of immigration authorities. When he left jail in 2009, hoping to return to school and his family, he was immediately collared by US Immigration and Customs Enforcement (ICE) for failing to apply for a green card at age fourteen.

One year after arriving in the United States, resettled refugees are required to apply for a green card or risk being deported as illegal immigrants. David claims he did not know this. His mother and father had acquired green cards, but they did not pick one up for him. When Human Rights Watch interviewed David in 2009, he had been sitting in a cell in Eloy, Arizona, for seven months. "I don't know when I can get out," David said. "I want to go back to Sacramento, go back to school. [My girlfriend] needs help with the kids. We just worry about day care and things the kids need."[35] David told Human Rights Watch that he never knew he was required to have a green card until he was placed in detention. His future was now in the hands of a judge.

The Process of Deportation

Normally, "unadjusted" refugees who are detained by ICE are set on the path to apply for green cards. However, the process can take anywhere from several months to a year, and the acquisition of a green card is not assured. Those who are denied approval undergo repatriation, the process of removing, or deporting, individuals from the United States and sending them back to their homelands. Human Rights Watch reports that "depending on the speed of the immigration court's docket, removal proceedings can last from 6 to 10 months, during which time the refugee is still required to remain in detention."[36] In 2013, the last year for which the department published statistics, the DHS had detained over 440,000 illegal immigrants like David Thomas. Those held were either captured at the border by the CBP or in the nation's interior by ICE. Some of those crossing from Mexico are caught and returned fairly quickly. "Returned" individuals are not formally charged and can make another attempt to cross the border without serious repercussions or even apply for legal entry. More commonly in recent years, border crossers and those captured deep inside the United States are charged with a misdemeanor or felony and brought before a judge who decides whether they should be removed from the country. If they are deported, removed individuals cannot apply to enter the country legally for a period of years (from three to twenty depending on the reason for removal) and any subsequent illegal entry will earn them deportation without a hearing.

A child soldier holds a gun during the Liberian civil war that took place in between 1997 and 2003. Liberians fleeing the war, including children wanting to avoid being forced to become soldiers, were granted resettlement privileges as refugees in the United States.

According to DHS statistics, the number of deportations has declined in recent years. In fact, ICE and CBP authorities have been focusing their efforts on those convicted of crimes or who are a threat to public safety or national security. This means that both organizations are prioritizing the turning back of recent unlawful entrants at the border and the nabbing of criminals and terrorist suspects who have managed to establish themselves in communities across the country. In 2015 ICE officers captured 69,478 individuals in the nation's interior. Of these, 65,539, or 91 percent, had been convicted of a crime. Of all the 235,413 persons removed from the country in 2015, 230,715, or 98 percent, met one of the DHS target priorities. Many more illegal entrants were returned without facing removal hearings. Those illegal immigrants who are not immediately returned are typically sent to any of the country's twenty-one DHS detention facilities to await removal proceedings, but because of overflow, numerous state and county facilities are also used.

In Detention

The DHS states that when illegal immigrants are placed in custody, they might be released with or without bail, or they can be detained pending further inquiry or removal. Any undocumented individual previously charged with a criminal offense—even if it was the crime of illegal entry—cannot post bond and will be detained pending felony charges. According to the DHS, Mexicans made up 56 percent of detainees in 2013; immigrants from Guatemala, Honduras, and El Salvador made up another 34 percent, while the remaining 10 percent came chiefly from Asia, Africa, South America, and the Caribbean. The DHS does not indicate how long a detainee can be held for deportation, only that "if an alien is ordered removed, the alien may be detained for a certain period of time pending repatriation."[37]

Human rights advocates argue that because the DHS offers no concrete timetable for removal, undocumented individuals can get stuck in detention facilities for many months. And while this process might not appear to be an unjust consequence of an illegal act, large numbers of these people have families and financial responsibilities that are severely disrupted by lengthy imprisonment. "Individuals who come back after being deported, or come back after being returned, primarily they're coming back for a reason," says Karen Lucas, a legislative associate at the American Immigration Lawyers Association. "Our system has been broken for so long that such a large percentage of the 11 million [undocumented people] really do have roots in this country."[38]

Amnesty International states that many of the undocumented people who get picked up and detained by CBP or ICE often do not know why they have been placed in holding, and many of these do not know what rights they have under both domestic and international law. Some are told that they can immediately end their detention by voluntarily deporting themselves and therefore avoid the criminal record that might result from a removal hearing. Amnesty International asserts that for those illegal immigrants who are fearful of authorities and might not speak the language well, accepting this offer can seem the easiest way out of their predicament "even though they may not have had an opportunity to consult with an attorney and they may not actually

> "Our system has been broken for so long that such a large percentage of the 11 million [undocumented people] really do have roots in this country."[38]
>
> —Karen Lucas, legislative associate at the American Immigration Lawyers Association

Illegal immigrants wait in a California detention center to be deported. According to the group Amnesty International, many such individuals are unaware of the rights they have under both domestic and international laws.

be deportable."[39] A 2012 report by the ACLU of Georgia claimed similar findings, alleging that removal officers and even immigration hearing judges were encouraging immigrants brought before them to sign "stipulated orders of removal," another term for voluntary deportation papers. According to the ACLU report, these orders were written in English, which many immigrants could not read adequately. In addition, the ACLU stated, "There were instances where deportation officers screamed at detainees who refused to sign stipulated orders of removal and threatened them with permanent detention" and two incidents in which officers "physically forced detainees to sign the order."[40] Such coercion is a violation of the right to due process protected by the Constitution and international human rights charters like the ICCPR and the Universal Declaration of Human Rights.

Isolation from Legal Aid

Both Amnesty International and the ACLU have conducted interviews with undocumented individuals and others involved in the detention and removal process who cite other practices that seem to deprive detainees of human rights. For example, many detainees end up in facilities that are removed from population centers where legal assistance or communication with the outside is available. Amnesty International insists:

> The ability to access the outside world is an essential safeguard against arbitrary detention. However, Amnesty International documented significant barriers immigrants face in accessing assistance and support while in detention. Problems included lack of access to legal counsel and consulates; lack of access to law libraries along with inadequate access to telephones; and frequent and sudden transfers of detainees to facilities located far away from courts, advocates, and family.[41]

While apprehended individuals are allowed to hire a lawyer to represent them at the removal hearing, those detainees in out-of-the-way places often cannot obtain such representation. According to the ACLU, even where legal services exist, detainees in the Georgia system were not notified of pro bono, or free, attorney organizations designed to help those who cannot pay. The ACLU noted that until 2011, the rules at one Georgia detention facility did not permit lawyers to personally visit clients who could afford to hire them.

Most undocumented immigrants end up representing themselves during removal hearings. Some report having little access in detention facilities to law libraries or computers that would enable them to obtain legal information. When brought to their hearings, those who do not speak English or cannot speak it well often have to struggle to understand the proceedings. Interpreters are not always provided at detention facilities or at hearings, and the ACLU of Georgia reported instances in which other immigrants—who were also unfamiliar with legal rights and court responsibilities—were asked to interpret for non-English speakers. The ACLU noted, "All of the facilities exhibited problems with detainees' access to legal information. At [one specific facility], none of the detainees interviewed

> "The ability to access the outside world is an essential safeguard against arbitrary detention."[41]
>
> —Amnesty International, a watchdog organization focused on protecting human rights

had been provided access to information about their basic legal rights."[42] Human rights advocates contend that such basic rights are guaranteed all accused persons. These guarantees appear in various international treaties that denounce arbitrary detention and insist on equality before the law as well as the implementation of fair and public trials.

Conditions of Detention

Article 5 of the Universal Declaration of Human Rights maintains that no one shall be subjected to cruel or inhuman treatment or punishment. Human rights advocates argue that the detention and processing of illegal immigrants in the United States often violates this and other international articles on the treatment of detainees. In the indictment of the Georgia detention system, the ACLU heard numerous complaints about the condition of cells, temperature extremes in the cells, overcrowding, and the poor quality of food and the serving of meals at unusual and inconsistent times. The organization also noted that facilities often ran out of hygiene products and that detainees simply went without. Perhaps more troubling, the ACLU of Georgia claimed, "detainees also face unreasonable delays in receiving medical care and in the case of detainees with mental disabilities, punitive rather than care-oriented treatment." Often detainees faced obstacles when they attempted to bring attention to such problems. According to the ACLU of Georgia, "Detainees who filed grievances did not always receive responses" and sometimes received "verbal and physical abuse, and retaliatory behavior from guards including placing detainees in segregation."[43]

Amnesty International claims that physical abuse in detention centers goes beyond retaliation against those who complain. It states that it has documented "inappropriate and excessive use of restraints"[44] on undocumented immigrant detainees. Other forms of abuse have also been reported. For instance, in 2014 women detainees in a Kansas City facility alleged that three employees engaged in sexual harassment and sexual abuse. Elise Foley of the *Huffington Post* says that a legal complaint launched by legal aid groups in the area noted examples in which women detainees were removed from their cells "for the purpose of engaging in sexual acts." The employees supposedly called the women "novias"

Deportations Focus on Illegal Immigrants Accused of Serious Crimes

The immigration resource website USimmigration.com reports that the Obama administration made it a priority to focus deportation efforts on illegal immigrants who committed serious crimes.

> New federal statistics are showing that, while deportations of small-time criminals and non-criminals are on the rise, so are the deportations of criminal aliens. Furthermore, as [former secretary of the] Department of Homeland Security Janet Napolitano has argued, many criminal aliens are currently serving prison sentences before they will be deported and therefore have not shown up in the statistics. Napolitano said, "The more serious offenders are still in prison. We're not going to see them reflected in the numbers until we can begin to remove them." In 2010, 392,862 illegal immigrants were deported. 195,772 of those were criminals of some kind or another. In fact, between 2008 and 2010, the deportation of criminal aliens increased by 71 percent from 114,415. . . . Corey Price, assistant field office director with ICE Enforcement and Removal Operations in Columbus, Ohio said, "Our focus in ICE is going after criminals. There are others who are here illegally that we also arrest, but our primary focus is on the worst of the worst."

USimmigration.com, "Criminal Alien Deportations on the Rise," 2011. www.usimmigration.com.

("sweethearts") and "girlfriends" and promised to help them and even give them money in return for sexual favors. Foley adds that a government spokesperson indicated that "ICE remains committed to ensuring all individuals in our custody are held and treated in a safe, secure and humane manner"[45] and that an investigation would be undertaken.

Deportation and Family Breakup

Whether suffering or not, illegal immigrant detainees wait in their cells until they either sign a stipulated order of removal or face a judge to contest deportation. The entire detention and subsequent deportation process is, according to human rights organizations, unjust. "Everyone has the right to liberty, freedom of movement, and the right not to be arbitrarily detained,"[46] Amnesty International claims. However, most governments and many observers of all political stripes maintain that deportation is not an unjust act. "The deportation of an immigrant illegally present in a nation is just, under any reasoned definition of just," asserts Paul Pauker in *American Thinker*. "The distinction made between citizens and noncitizens is a fundamental aspect of every nation."[47] Yet it is not always the act of deportation that upsets those critics who are concerned with human rights, but rather the consequences of the act.

Chief among these concerns is the breakup of family units. Article 23 of the ICCPR states, "The family is the natural and fundamental group unit of society and is entitled to protection by society and the State."[48] Human rights activists argue that detention and deportation violate this trust. In many instances of arrest, parents who might be in the country illegally are separated from their children, who may be US citizens by birth. The parents may end up in detention and removal proceedings for weeks or months, leaving their kids stranded or in foster care. The Center for American Progress published a report in 2012 that examined the debilitating effects of deportation on families. In it, author Joanna Dreby notes, "A recent report by the Applied Research Council estimates that at least 5,100 children are currently in the U.S. foster care system and cannot be reunited with their parents due to a parent's detention or deportation—and 15,000 more could face similar circumstances in the next five years."[49] The wait can be grueling for mothers and fathers. "A 34-year-old Mexican mother of three told Amnesty International that she was arrested at her home in front of her 3-year-old autistic US citizen son by local police and jailed for 24 days," the organization reports. "After nearly three weeks in detention with no indication of when she would be able to return to her family, she tried to kill herself."[50] Other organizations provide similar portraits of detainee mothers and fathers desperate with worry over the fate of their children.

In 2011 and again in 2014, President Barack Obama ordered a review of deportation policies with the intent of focusing less

> "The deportation of an immigrant illegally present in a nation is just, under any reasoned definition of just. The distinction made between citizens and noncitizens is a fundamental aspect of every nation."[47]
>
> —Paul Pauker, blog writer for the *American Thinker* website

Facing deportation proceedings, parents who are in the United States illegally may be separated from their children, who are citizens by birth. Activists argue that this violates the concept that the family unit is entitled to protection from society and from the government.

on families and more on criminals. However, observers claim the detention and deportation of noncriminal illegals have not slowed significantly. The societal and personal impact of these policies is staggering, human rights advocates assert. Dreby claims that because more detainees are male than female, deportation creates large numbers of single mothers who are left to care for children, and as a consequence, "children in single-parent households are 4.2 times more likely to live in poverty than are children with married parents." While Dreby goes on to say that many families do reunite either in their countries of origin or in the United States, "one-quarter were unable to," permanently forcing many into poverty and leaving emotional scars on both children and adults. Even those who reunite can face long-lasting problems, "as financial and emotional hardships rarely vanish even after the immediate trauma of such an event,"[51] Dreby notes.

Law Versus Liberty

Many of the concerns regarding the treatment of detainees and their potential deportation seem to conflict with the government's

Deportations Do Not Focus on Illegal Immigrants Accused of Serious Crimes

New York Times reporters Ginger Thompson and Sarah Cohen state that Barack Obama's deportation efforts were not targeting hardened criminals; instead, many of those deported were arrested for minor crimes.

> The president has said the government is going after "criminals, gang bangers, people who are hurting the community, not after students, not after folks who are here just because they're trying to figure out how to feed their families."

> But a *New York Times* analysis of internal government records shows that since President Obama took office, two-thirds of the nearly two million deportation cases involve people who had committed minor infractions, including traffic violations, or had no criminal record at all. Twenty percent—or about 394,000—of the cases involved people convicted of serious crimes, including drug-related offenses, the records show. . . .

> Mr. Obama came to office promising comprehensive immigration reform, but lacking sufficient support, the administration took steps it portrayed as narrowing the focus of enforcement efforts on serious criminals. Yet the records show that the enforcement net actually grew, picking up more and more immigrants with minor or no criminal records.

Ginger Thompson and Sarah Cohen, "More Deportations Follow Minor Crimes, Data Shows," *New York Times*, April 7, 2014, p. A1.

stated commitment to protect human rights. Some policy makers and enforcement representatives maintain that the nation is trying its best to apply its laws to the huge numbers of border crossers as well as the millions of undocumented persons already living in American communities. To them, comprehensive immigration reform is the answer, not a rejection of the nation's right to enforce its borders. Some even believe that the work of human rights groups is counterproductive to bringing about more meaningful immigration reform. D.A. King, president of the Dustin Inman Society, a group in Georgia that advocates border security, asserts that the ACLU's report on detention facilities was misleading because it relied too much on the obviously biased testimony of immigrants. King claims the ACLU "is leading the anti-enforcement charge here in Georgia. . . . Their goal here is to stop any enforcement of U.S. immigration law."[52]

Human rights groups like the ACLU insist, however, that the United States must act as a more responsible global citizen by making sure that its laws conform to the progressive politics of leading nations. In addition, these groups argue that the government must prove its commitment to due process and impartial treatment of all people within its borders as a testimony to its own ideals. As Denise Gilman, a law professor at the University of Texas, explains, "Human rights law analysis should . . . spur positive changes to immigration detention in the United States that will bring rationality back to our system and protect liberty."[53]

Whether such aims will sway policy makers is uncertain. In an era of terror threats, controversial welfare spending, and economic instability, 61 percent of American voters polled by Rasmussen Reports in February 2016 believed that the government was not being aggressive enough in deporting those who are in the country illegally. It remains to be seen, though, how the government—spurred on by the will of the people—will balance the interests of national sovereignty against a concern for the human rights of immigrants who knowingly and purposefully violate that sovereignty.

Chapter 4

Human Trafficking

Focus Questions

1. Do you believe America's immigration system is in any way responsible for the human trafficking of illegal immigrants? Why or why not?

2. Do you believe the US government is doing enough to stop human trafficking involving illegal immigrants and to assist those who have fallen victim to traffickers? Explain your answer.

3. What factors make undocumented immigrants more vulnerable to human traffickers, and how should these factors be addressed by government and law enforcement?

According to the US Department of State, about 14,500 to 17,500 men, women, and children are victims of human trafficking in the United States each year. These numbers place the United States low on the list of countries known for trafficking in human beings. The federal government passed the Trafficking Victims Protection Act (TVPA) in 2000 and has since reauthorized the act a few times to show a commitment to preventing this crime and prosecuting anyone engaged in it. Despite meeting the standards established by the act, the United States still battles human trafficking. For example, between June 2010 and June 2012, law enforcement in California, one of the largest sites of human trafficking in the nation, identified over twelve hundred victims and arrested nearly eighteen hundred perpetrators involved in this crime. In a 2013 article for the Institute for Policy Studies, Tiffany Williams claims that "human trafficking is a pervasive problem in the United States that continues to thrive as a modern-day form of slavery in dozens of industries and sectors."[54]

The same year that the United States adopted the TVPA, the UN put forth its Convention Against Transnational Organized Crime, a list of protocols that went into effect in 2003 and included measures to fight human trafficking. Both the UN and the US government acknowledge that human trafficking typically assumes two forms. The first is the harboring, transport, or coercion of individuals for the purposes of forced labor or debt bondage. The second involves compelling individuals to commit sexual acts for profit through force or fraud. While anyone can be a victim of either of these forms, UN and US authorities recognize that immigrant populations—especially undocumented immigrants—are particularly vulnerable to human trafficking. The two issues are hard to separate, even in the United States. As Williams asserts, "While exact numbers are notoriously difficult to calculate, the degree of overlap between undocumented immigration and human trafficking is thought to be significant. This overlap creates challenges for a government that tries to both combat undocumented immigration and simultaneously identify and help victims of human trafficking."[55]

> "While exact numbers are notoriously difficult to calculate, the degree of overlap between undocumented immigration and human trafficking is thought to be significant."[55]
>
> —Tiffany Williams, associate director of the Institute for Policy Studies

Victimizing Undocumented Immigrants

The Federation for American Immigration Reform (FAIR) explains that illegal immigrants fall victim to human trafficking for a variety of reasons. These include the facts that they are isolated from the support of their home communities, their illegal status allows traffickers to easily coerce or manipulate them, and their limited language skills and their financial need make them dependent on others for assistance navigating life in a new land. Typically, the traffickers are of the same nationality or ethnicity as their victims and thus can appear more helpful than foreigners or other outsiders. FAIR states that illegal immigrants "are often victimized by traffickers from a similar ethnic or national background, on whom they may be dependent for employment or support in the foreign country."[56] According to a 2014 report from the US Department of State, the majority of undocumented individuals caught up in human trafficking operations come from Mexico, the Philippines, Thailand, Honduras, Guatemala, India, and El Salvador.

Some of the traffickers run highly organized networks that target immigrants who are impoverished and desperate for US jobs that pay good wages. A 2014 report by the Texas Department of Public Safety, for example, maintains that Mexican drug cartels either operate or facilitate the operation of most human trafficking organizations along the southern US border. In other parts of the county, criminal groups and crooked employers likewise entice immigrants from around the world to illegally enter the country. All traffickers typically promise that they can both provide safe passage into the country and secure work for the immigrants once they arrive. In reality, the traffickers commonly use the immigrants' undocumented status as a form of black-

President George W. Bush signs into law the Trafficking Victims Protection Reauthorization Act in 2005. Isolated and usually without financial resources, illegal immigrants are particularly vulnerable to falling victim to human trafficking.

PREVENTING
HUMAN TRAFFICKIN

mail, holding individuals until they can pay off the debt they incurred for the services rendered.

Sex Trafficking

In 2005 a huge sex trafficking ring in Houston, Texas, was broken up by federal authorities. Roughly 120 undocumented women were rescued from a network of traffickers who forced their victims to work in cantinas as prostitutes, picking up men six or seven nights a week. Lisa Olsen of the *Houston Chronicle* reported that "for years, the ring preyed on women and girls from Honduras, El Salvador, Nicaragua and Guatemala, illegally bringing them to Houston with false promises of legitimate work and then forcing them to work in cantinas to pay off smuggling fees from $8,000 to $15,000—as well as all living expenses." According to Olsen's article, authorities who raided the bars "found detailed ledgers and notebooks showing how victims had been billed for everything they ate and drank, for their rent, for their clothes, for their transport to the U.S. and for shipping money back home."[57] One of the victims told the paper, "I had to do everything that [the ringleaders] said—they had a camera outside my apartment that recorded everything."[58]

Although in this instance the undocumented individuals were women, it is not uncommon for traffickers to convince parents to allow their underage children to make the crossing. On the other side of the border, these boys and girls are then held in sexual slavery, far from the help of their parents. A 2016 Legal Immigrants for America news article recounts the story of Ana Maria, a young girl from Nicaragua who wanted to escape political turmoil in her country. Her mother, who had already made the crossing into the United States, paid a coyote, or smuggler, to bring across her daughter. Instead, the coyote pocketed the fee and delivered the young girl into a house of prostitution in Arizona. According to the article, "Many other sex slaves were in the house with Ana Maria, including little girls as young as 8 years old."[59] There, Ana Maria spent eleven years and ended up having a baby with one of her

> "Many other sex slaves were in the house . . . , including little girls as young as 8 years old."[59]
>
> —Legal Immigrants for America, an organization promoting legal immigration organization

clients. A little older and wiser, Ana Maria fled her captors with her child, suffering a gunshot wound during her escape. She was picked up by Arizonans and handed over to authorities, who put her under protection until she could legally apply for citizenship.

Slave Labor

Other undocumented immigrants are trafficked into businesses that exploit their labor. Many have no familiarity with America, suffer from poor English language skills, and fear being turned in to authorities. Because of this they are more likely to submit to inhuman living conditions, substandard wages, and unjust confinement at the hands of sweatshop operators or other unscrupulous business owners. In a 2014 report, the Texas Department of Public Safety told of a sting that nabbed two business referral operations in Houston that trafficked in illegal workers from Central America and Mexico. The businesses advertised in Chinese newspapers as providing take-out and delivery services for Chinese restaurants, "but instead of delivering food, they delivered illegal aliens already in the US to restaurant owners and managers looking for cheap labor." The report went on to say:

> The victims worked twelve hours a day, six days a week, and were not permitted to receive tips or get paid overtime. They were not provided any insurance benefits, food safety training, health examinations, or job training, and they were paid far less than the minimum wage. Additionally, the business operators provided unfavorable living arrangements either at their residence or at another off-site residential location; 18 people were housed in a 2,000-square-foot house, for example.[60]

In 2013 fourteen 7-Eleven convenience stores were cited by federal prosecutors for operating a slavery ring in New York and Virginia. Authorities under the DHS conducted investigations of 7-Elevens throughout the region and found the accused franchise operators had lured fifty illegal Pakistani and Filipino immigrants to the United States to run their stores. The immigrants were given fake identification that had been stolen from US citi-

Opening the Southern Border Is the Solution to Stopping Human Trafficking

Sirenia Jimenez, an attorney in California, insists that opening the US-Mexico border will help end human trafficking because illegal immigrants will no longer have to use smugglers' agreements to cross between countries.

> An open border would minimize racial discrimination against migrants and reduce deaths of and violence against those migrants—both of which would alleviate the harming of their dignity and help them feel more secure. Giving migrants an identity and making them aware that they have been given protection in both countries, Mexico and the United States, will minimize migrants' susceptibility to crime because they will now have both governments to support them and give them outlets to seek that protection. In addition, they can skip the dangerous route through Mexico, where many of their abuses occur, and fly directly into the United States. Lastly, they will no longer have to seek "coyotes," who oftentimes take advantage of migrants, in order to come into the country because their entrance will be legal.

Sirenia Jimenez, "The Route of Death for Central and South American Illegal Immigrants Can Come to an End with a Change in the United States' Policy," *Global Business & Development Law Journal*, September 10, 2012, pp. 468–69.

zens, including deceased persons and kids. They were forced to live in substandard housing owned by the franchise operators. Their wages were also substandard, ranging from $300 to $500 for one hundred hours of work time per week. According to the authorities, the arrangement had been going on since 2000, and the owners had made roughly $180 million off the labor of these undocumented workers.

Prosecuting Traffickers and Helping Victims

The DHS and its offices are involved in rooting out human traffickers in the United States. These agencies are granted the power to arrest human traffickers because debt servitude and other forms of slavery are specifically outlawed by section 18 of the US Code. Parts of this section have existed for some time, and others have more recently been amended by the passage of the TVPA. Together these parts of the code make forced labor and sex trafficking unlawful. In addition, they criminalize the act of holding persons against their will or harboring or transporting such individuals. In addition, in 2010 the DHS launched the Blue Campaign to increase public awareness about human trafficking and to help law enforce-

Department of Homeland Security official Maria Odom discusses the Blue Campaign with law enforcement officers. The campaign is intended to educate the public about human trafficking and assist authorities in investigating and prosecuting this crime.

ment investigate this crime and pursue those criminals involved. According to the DHS, the department and its agents take "a victim-centered approach to combat human trafficking, which places equal value on identifying and stabilizing victims and on investigating and prosecuting traffickers."[61] The DHS, along with the US Department of Justice and the US Department of Health and Human Services, also instituted the Federal Strategic Action Plan on Services for Victims of Human Trafficking in the United States, 2013–2017 to coordinate efforts between these departments and expand services to victims of human trafficking.

Like all criminal victims, individuals who have suffered at the hands of human traffickers are given medical and psychiatric evaluations and care. Sexually abused or battered persons are afforded counseling and protection, and all victims are put up in secure locations until their stories can be told and perhaps help in the arrest and indictment of the traffickers. Most significantly, the TVPA authorized visas for the victims of human trafficking in order to secure their help in investigating and prosecuting crimes. U Visas grant temporary nonimmigrant status to victims who have suffered substantial criminal abuse. T Visas provide nonimmigrant status to victims of human trafficking not only for their assistance in criminal investigations but also to help these individuals rebuild their lives. T Visas even permit their holders to access health care and food assistance programs. Both U and T Visas can be extended for up to four years, after which time these undocumented persons can follow normal procedures to apply for legal immigrant or citizen status. Although these aspects of victim assistance are still in practice, the TVPA was not reauthorized in 2013, leaving many fearful that government commitment to victims of human trafficking was in jeopardy.

Safeguarding the Human Rights of Victims

While the DHS insists that it is focused on protecting trafficking victims, human rights activists are among those who are worried about the federal government's guarantees and its specific interests. For example, some claim the government is treating rescued individuals as illegal immigrants first and victims second.

In a July 2014 letter to Barack Obama, Human Rights Watch claimed that children were routinely interrogated by armed and uniformed members of the CBP about possible victimization, instead of being placed in a safe environment with qualified professionals who can better address such sensitive topics. Human Rights Watch believes such practices are part of the government's ramping up of expedited removals, the deportation of individuals without a hearing. There are additional concerns that those of any age who qualify for temporary visas are used by the government to prosecute cases and then released back back into the broken immigration system to potentially await deportation.

Perhaps more worrisome are the claims that the US Department of Health and Human Services is not careful in handing over unaccompanied minors to appropriate protective environments. Many undocumented young people—whether caught in human trafficking rings or not—are routinely released to relatives to await hearings. However, kinship claims are not investigated thoroughly, observers claim. In 2014 this lack of oversight proved disastrous. A loophole in immigration policy permitted Mexican minors to be deported without a hearing, but "Other than Mexican" immigrants were allowed to stay while awaiting judgment. Central American human trafficking cartels used the loophole to flood the southern border with undocumented young people from Guatemala, El Salvador, and Honduras, who fell for scams to exploit the law and find promised work on the other side. Once these young people were placed on backlogged hearing schedules, they were handed over to individuals claiming to be relatives in the United States. "Turns out that quite a few were being handed off to the criminal syndicates that specialize in human slavery," *Investor's Business Daily* reports. "A study by the Center for American Progress points out more than half of the unaccompanied minors were teenage boys, and less than a third were looking to reunite with relatives. The study suggests that the traffickers' false promises of (non-slave) work lured them."[62]

Human rights advocates are very concerned about protecting the rights of trafficking victims. They are outraged over the inhumane conditions that victims face during their journey

UN officials open a conference in Italy in 2010. The meeting led to the adoption of the organization's Convention Against Transnational Organized Crime. Among other types of crime, the convention targeted human trafficking and dictated how victims should be treated.

RESENTATIVE OF THE
PETARY-GENERAL

PRESIDENT

and their enslavement. They would also like to see the United States do more to ensure that the human rights of victims are not violated after their rescue. Beyond the requirements of its own laws, the US government is bound to protect victims of human trafficking and prosecute traffickers because it has signed the UN Convention Against Transnational Organized Crime and other international antitrafficking measures. Such agreements dictate that victims be given adequate housing, medical and psychological care, and opportunities for minors to continue their education.

Critics believe that because the United States places its own laws above international agreements, human rights concerns may get overlooked in the handling of victims. Even worse, critics fear that the government might focus on the illegal status

Securing the Southern Border Is the Solution to Stopping Human Trafficking

Brandon Darby is the Breitbart Texas managing director, and Bob Price serves as associate editor and senior political news contributor for Breitbart News. These authors maintain that leaving the US-Mexico border unsecured invites human traffickers to ply their trade.

Many of the most caring people in the U.S. think they are helping the poor from Latin America by leaving our Southwest border wide open between ports-of-entry, but they are not. Several of the transnational criminal organizations (cartels) operating in Central America and Mexico make an estimated one-third or more of their profits from illegal immigration. Specifically, two groups below Texas, the Gulf and Los Zetas cartels, are largely fueled by the trafficking and smuggling of human beings.

The brutality of these criminal groups, from incinerating innocents in a network of ovens to their near complete control of state and local governments, is largely paid for by funds generated from illegal immigration—a shadowy economic engine that is only possible because we refuse to properly secure our border with Mexico.

Brandon Darby and Bob Price, "Rape Trees, Dead Migrants and the Consequences of an Open Border," Breitbart News, April 25, 2016. www.breitbart.com.

of these victims and seek to prosecute them instead of providing them with humanitarian assistance. For instance, many minors working for sex traffickers are forced into prostitution. When picked up by authorities as part of a prostitution and trafficking ring, these underage persons may be labeled as criminals because they worked as prostitutes and may be fast-tracked through the deportation process. This problem was apparently common enough by 2012 for the UN to warn the United States and other countries to realign their procedures with international law. In a report on human trafficking in June of that year, Joy Ngozi Ezeilo, the UN special rapporteur on trafficking (an investigator sanctioned by the UN), stated, "Indeed, criminalization and/or detention of victims of trafficking is incompatible with a rights-based approach to trafficking because it inevitably compounds the harm already experienced by trafficked persons and denies them the rights to which they are entitled."[63]

A Matter of Focus

While the UN and various human rights groups call for a greater emphasis on protecting the human rights of trafficking victims, some commentators believe the emphasis is misplaced. They argue that it is a porous border that encourages human trafficking, and they insist that stronger immigration policies are needed to deter border crossing and punish those who violate proper immigration rules. For example, although FAIR has noted several tragic instances of human trafficking in the past decade, it maintains that "a critical strategy in ending human trafficking is better enforcement of our immigration laws and greater federal-local cooperation in law enforcement."[64] However, critics assert that enforcement must be tempered with compassion and that while illegal immigrants are vulnerable to human trafficking schemes, the crime of trafficking must be the focus of prosecution and not the undocumented status of its victims.

> "Criminalization and/or detention of victims of trafficking is incompatible with a rights-based approach to trafficking because it inevitably compounds the harm already experienced by trafficked persons and denies them the rights to which they are entitled."[63]
>
> —Joy Ngozi Ezeilo, UN special rapporteur on trafficking

Chapter 5

Policies and Prevention Efforts

Focus Questions

1. When people enter the country illegally or overstay their visas, what rights should they have while in this country, and why?

2. Is the United States doing enough to ensure that the human rights of illegal immigrants are not violated? Explain your answer.

3. Should the United States grant amnesty to illegal immigrants? Would amnesty benefit America or harm it? Explain your answers.

In 2012 and again in 2014, Barack Obama used his executive order privilege to enact immigration policy that would help shield families from deportation. The 2012 Deferred Action for Childhood Arrivals (DACA) policy exempted from deportation all illegal immigrants who were under age thirty-one and claimed to have entered the country before their sixteenth birthday. In 2014 Obama expanded coverage to those who entered the country as a child before 2010 regardless of current age. Also in 2014, Obama announced the Deferred Action for Parents of Americans and Lawful Permanent Residents to delay deportation of parents of children covered by DACA. According to the White House, the two programs would protect about 5 million undocumented immigrants from deportation.

Despite the forgiveness shown in these executive actions, the president has been responsible for more deportations than previous administrations. Over Obama's term, the DHS has removed more than 2 million individuals from the country. The president has rationalized these deportation numbers by insisting that enforcement officers are narrowly targeting known criminals, suspected terrorists, and recent border crossers. In a June 2015 speech, Secretary of Homeland Security Jeh Johnson affirmed this, stating, "We are making it clear that we should not expend our limited resources on deporting those who have been here for years, have committed no serious crimes and have, in effect, become integrated members of our society. . . . These people are here, they live among us, and they are not going away."[65] According to a July 2015 article in the *Washington Post*, Johnson has also said the president's mandate to go after high-priority targets extends to the over four hundred thousand undocumented individuals in US detention facilities. DHS officials have noted that about three thousand people have been released from such facilities or had the charges against them dropped.

The president's policies suggest that his administration is lenient toward illegal immigrants. Because of this apparent stance, opponents have been quick to stall his plans. In 2015 twenty-six states won a federal lawsuit to put Obama's expansion of DACA on hold. Still, the DHS and its agencies are supposedly following the spirit of the president's orders. The US Department of Justice is heading the administration's legal appeal, with a spokesperson announcing in November 2015 that the department "remains committed to taking steps that will resolve the immigration litigation as quickly as possible in order to allow DHS to bring greater accountability to our immigration system by prioritizing the removal of the worst offenders, not people who have long ties to the United States and who are raising American children."[66]

Refugees or Illegal Immigrants?

Among those most recently targeted for removal, however, are the more than two hundred thousand individuals who fled increasing gang violence in Central America in 2014. Of these, roughly fifty thousand were unaccompanied children whose parents sent them north to take advantage of the DACA amnesty for minors. To stem the influx, Obama met with Mexican president Enrique Nieto in June of that year to develop a plan to address what the White House termed a humanitarian crisis. In July Mexico announced its *Programa Frontera Sur* (or southern border program)

President Barack Obama speaks with a young beneficiary of his Deferred Action for Childhood Arrivals policy, which he enacted by executive order in 2012. The policy exempted from deportation all undocumented immigrants under age thirty-one who claimed to have arrived in the country before their sixteenth birthday.

to crack down on immigrants from Honduras, El Salvador, and Guatemala who were using railways and other entry points to make the trip north through Mexico. Large numbers—including many children—who traveled these common paths were turned back to their homelands, where they faced uncertain futures.

In a 2016 *New York Times* article, Nicholas Kristof described how well the *Programa Frontera Sur* was working. He tells the story of Cristóbal, a sixteen-year-old Honduran immigrant who had experienced the violence of drug gangs firsthand and was caught fleeing across the border between Mexico and his homeland. "If I'm sent back, they will kill me,"[67] Cristóbal says of the gang that forced him to serve as a cocaine runner at age fourteen. According to Kristof, Cristóbal only dared to make his escape after witnessing the murder of two of his friends. He awaits possible deportation in a youth camp set up by the Mexican government to deal with the lone children caught along the border.

The White House claims the Mexican government developed the plan to deal with the crisis on its own, but human rights workers and commentators like Kristof are convinced otherwise. Kristof reports that the United States gave Mexico $86 million to support the program—an act of bribery, he claims. Maureen Meyer, a senior associate for migrant rights at the Washington Office on Latin America, a human rights advocacy group, agrees. In a 2015 article for *In These Times*, Meyer said, "I think it is clear that, last summer, the U.S. pressured Mexico to increase these efforts [to crack down on migration] as a way to help them deal with the 'problem' of Central Americans flooding into South Texas."[68] Kristof remarks that this method of helping "betrays some of the world's most vulnerable people."[69]

To many like Kristof and Meyer, the cross-border movement of the Central Americans is a refugee crisis, not a matter of illegal immigration. According to them, the humanitarian response would be to view these individuals—both in Mexico and in the United States—as asylum seekers. Instead, Obama and Nieto both worked to return the Central Americans to their homelands. Human Rights Watch reports that less than 1 percent of the child refugees in Mexico have been granted asylum. In America, ICE—under Obama's orders—began conducting raids on the residences of the Central Americans who made it across the US-Mexico border. In early 2016 ICE operatives in Georgia, Texas, and North Carolina nabbed 121 individuals who were subject to deportation. Again, the government insists that those targeted were illegal immigrants with criminal records. Critics argue that many of the arrested are part of families that have made the journey in order to find protection from the gang life they left behind. Cecillia Wang, director of the ACLU's Immigrants' Rights Project, claims, "The administration is doubling down on a system that is rigged against these families." She insists that families are being torn apart because the US government is hurrying to dispel these immigrants rather than listening to their pleas. "Many . . . had no lawyers because they could not afford them," Wang continues. "Without counsel, traumatized refugees don't understand what is happening in court and cannot get their legitimate asylum claim heard."[70]

Treatment at the Border

Human rights advocates do not believe all undocumented individuals are seeking asylum in America and therefore should automatically be granted government protections. However, most do contend that America's policies should not punish immigrants or force them to return to the chaos and turmoil from which they might have escaped. Human Rights Watch recommends that the CBP reform its conduct regulations and make sure all undocumented individuals in detention facilities are heard and any fears expressed about returning home be taken seriously. In its 2015 statement to the US Commission on Civil Rights, Human Rights Watch made an even bolder request of the border patrol and its treatment of the thousands of Central Americans who have crossed the southern border in recent years: "CBP, until it undertakes these reforms, should apply a presumption of fear of return for migrants from Honduras, El Salvador, Guatemala and other countries experiencing similar conditions."[71]

In addition, Human Rights Watch has called on the Obama administration to stop expedited removals and to eliminate the detention of children. In a 2014 article on the border screening process, the organization stated, "International law prohibits the detention of migrant children and discourages the detention of asylum seekers. Detention interferes with individuals' ability to assert claims to asylum, access counsel, and harms the physical and mental health of children as they struggle with life behind bars and the uncertainties of indefinite detention."[72] The organization believes that immigrant families should be provided with alternate housing because detention facilities are unpleasant, overcrowded, and possibly home to abusive guards and detained criminals.

The CBP insists its operations always conform to the law and that its officers are well trained in dealing with the public and any-

> "International law prohibits the detention of migrant children and discourages the detention of asylum seekers."[72]
>
> —Human Rights Watch, an international organization that advocates for human rights

In compliance with the Programa Frontera Sur, *Mexican officials halt a train carrying Central American immigrants—many of them children—fleeing violence in their home countries. Critics charge that the United States helped fund the program to stem the flow of Central American immigrants across the border of South Texas.*

one suspected of trespassing on US soil. The CBP has internal review policies and has established a way for anyone to register a complaint with the office on its website. In a May 2016 response to alleged poor treatment of undocumented immigrants and legal foreign visitors in both Texas and New Mexico, the CBP issued a statement that emphasized its continuing commitment to professionalism: "CBP provides ongoing training in customer service and professionalism at the entry-level, and throughout an officer's career and has a robust Professionalism Service Manager program with dedicated officers covering all operational environments to specifically handle professionalism-related issues and concerns which are highlighted via posters and outreach at all ports of entry."[73]

CBP commissioner R. Gil Kerlikowske praised the conduct of his officers for their handling of the many unaccompanied minors from Central America who fell into their care. "I have seen CBP employees respond to these difficulties with professionalism and

Executive Actions Subvert the Rule of Law

David Inserra, a policy analyst at the Heritage Foundation, says that presidential efforts to exempt illegal immigrants from US laws is disrespectful and tyrannical.

> As The Heritage Foundation has outlined, the "President cannot effectively amend a law by exempting entire categories of lawbreakers from the application of that law, particularly if done for political or policy reasons." The Administration's current non-enforcement of U.S. immigration laws damages the U.S.'s commitment to these principles of the rule of law: Illegal immigrants are not accountable for the laws they have broken; the law is manipulated and contorted to no longer be fair or understood; and the Administration's legal process applies the law unevenly depending on current "enforcement priorities." While non-enforcement may be a desired (but unwise) political or policy objective by certain groups or individuals, to ignore the law, which was passed by Congress and signed into law by a President, based on the Administration's current preference is no different in principle than the absolute monarchs of old or the tyrants of today.

David Inserra, "Ten-Step Checklist for Revitalizing America's Immigration System: How the Administration Can Fulfill Its Responsibilities," Heritage Foundation Special Report #160, November 3, 2014. www.heritage.org.

compassion," Kerlikowske said. "They've made heroic efforts with these children; rescuing them and caring for them in the most humane and compassionate way. I am extremely proud of their dedication and of how they have risen to this challenge."[74] However, even as the organization acknowledges the professional performance of its duties in the managing of so many children, it stresses that it will continue to curb illegal entries and discourage those who would seek to make such dangerous crossings into US territory.

Preserving Moral Safeguards

For those already living in the United States—perhaps for years or even decades, human rights advocates and their critics also debate policy and its outcomes. Some advocates, like Joseph Carens, a political science professor at the University of Toronto in Canada, believe that all governments should aspire to the moral high ground. Carens is an American by birth and a supporter of a pathway to citizenship for illegals in the United States. He says that the government and the public should weigh the moral imperatives of this issue. In an interview in the *New York Times*, Carens states that even if Americans feel it is morally appropriate to bar some people from entering the country or to partake of its social services, they still must compare that to the morality of forcing those people to live underground and in fear for the rest of their lives. "Living and working in a society makes immigrants members of that society over time, even if they arrived and settled without permission," Carens argues. "So it would be morally wrong to kick them out. We should give them status as permanent residents with the normal access to citizenship that this allows."[75]

However, even if a pathway to citizenship is not an option at present, human rights defenders believe the government must respect its commitment to global human rights in the treatment of the undocumented. In a document published in 2012, Amnesty International makes several recommendations to both the federal and state governments in preserving human rights even as they hunt for illegals, conduct raids, and carry out deportations. The organization demands the end of racial profiling and any tolerance for discrimination among ICE, CBP, or DHS personnel. It also recommends that "the Department of Homeland Security's Office of Inspector General should immediately conduct and complete thorough reviews of all relevant immigration enforcement programs . . . to determine whether they are resulting in racial profiling and/or other human rights violations."[76]

> "Living and working in a society makes immigrants members of that society over time, even if they arrived and settled without permission."[75]
>
> —Joseph Carens, political science professor at the University of Toronto

Amnesty International and other rights organizations also maintain that detention and deportation should be humane and considerate of the rights of the detainees. They recommend that detention take into account a concern for the separation of families, the imprisoning of children, and the health and education of those who must wait behind bars for a hearing. They also demand that all instances of reported or suspected abuse by guards be investigated thoroughly. Furthermore, these organizations insist that deportation judges be provided with all the facts in a case and consider the length of an immigrant's ties to the United States to make informed decisions and not be pressured to expedite removals.

Inconsistent Policies and Actions

So far, the federal government has not taken steps to address these issues. The DHS and its agencies maintain that they are following the rules established for the rounding up, detention, and deportation of undocumented persons. They contend that they are also taking steps to ensure their officers are not jeopardizing anyone in their care or within their jurisdiction. For example, the victim-centered approach of the DHS's Blue Campaign suggests a concern for illegal immigrants that goes beyond simple deportation. The CBP also made headlines in 2016 for posting a "sensitive locations" policy on its website. The policy dictates that officers cannot independently take action against suspects in places of worship, schools, medical facilities, or during public rallies or parades. Only in extreme emergencies or through approval of a supervisor can agents break this rule. Several commentators called the posting an attempt to help undocumented immigrants find sanctuary and elude capture. They blame the adoption and posting of such policies on the Obama administration, insisting that the administration's stance on border security is making it hard for law enforcement to do its job. "This administration has systematically and maliciously attacked and deconstructed all phases of border enforcement," Dan Stein, president of FAIR, told Fox News. "It's to the point now where virtually nobody has to go home."[77]

> "This administration has systematically and maliciously attacked and deconstructed all phases of border enforcement. It's to the point now where virtually nobody has to go home."[77]
>
> —Dan Stein, president of FAIR

Immigration enforcement agencies may often be blamed for bad policy, but they do not make the rules. Congress deliberates on and enacts immigration legislation. So far, immigration reform has yet to occur. Liberal politicians blame a Republican-controlled

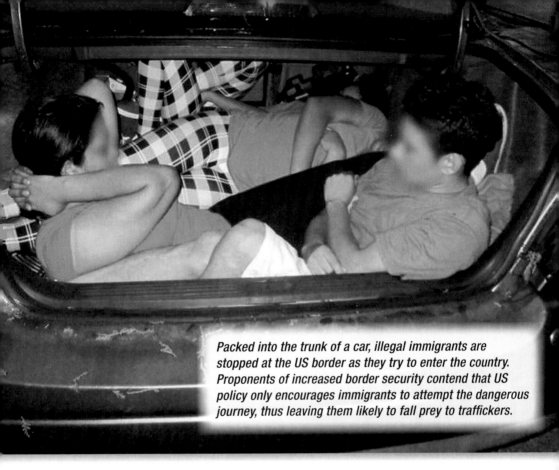

Packed into the trunk of a car, illegal immigrants are stopped at the US border as they try to enter the country. Proponents of increased border security contend that US policy only encourages immigrants to attempt the dangerous journey, thus leaving them likely to fall prey to traffickers.

House and Senate for foot-dragging. Conservative politicians maintain that reform must not compromise national security or cheapen citizenship by abandoning the legal immigration process. In the interim, current laws appear obsolete or unevenly applied, and abuse and tragedy seem more common when the federal government has no clear goal in mind.

Some conservative commentators claim that Obama's seeming disinterest in strengthening the border is worsening human rights abuses against immigrants. Ray Walser, Jena Baker McNeill, and Jessica Zuckerman of the Heritage Foundation wrote a paper in 2011, a year before the president enacted DACA, to point fingers at the "inconsistent policy by the Obama Administration, which downplays the risks of illegal migration, and an unorganized U.S. border security strategy." According to the authors, illegal immigrants face harsh—even deadly—environments on their journeys and along the way often become the victims of "kidnapping, robbery, extortion, sexual violence, and death at the hands of cartels, smugglers, and even corrupt Mexican government officials."

Executive Actions Do Not Subvert the Rule of Law

Ilya Somin, a law professor at George Mason University, argues that moral considerations can influence presidential action without destroying the rule of law. He believes that presidents have often used broad discretion in deciding which crimes federal law enforcement will and will not prosecute. Like others before him, Obama is justified in implementing such discretion in order to aid immigrants.

> To the extent that large-scale use of prosecutorial discretion is ever appropriate, it is surely so in the case of helping people whose only violation of the law is fleeing poverty and oppression under terrible Third World governments. Few other offenders have such a compelling moral justification for breaking the law. I strongly support the legalization of marijuana and the abolition of the War on Drugs more generally. But illegal immigrants violating the law to escape Third World conditions are considerably more deserving of our compassion than college students violating it to experiment with marijuana or other illegal drugs. If exemption from prosecution is acceptable for the latter, it should be permitted for the former too. . . .
>
> Long before today, presidential administrations unavoidably had to make broad discretionary decisions about which of the many violations of federal law out there are worth prosecuting and which ones are not. And long before today, those decisions were influenced by policy and moral considerations.

Ilya Somin, "Obama, Immigration, and the Rule of Law," *Washington Post*, November 20, 2014. www.washingtonpost.com.

Walser, McNeill, and Zuckerman add, "Exacerbating the problem is that enforcement of immigration laws inside the United States has been inconsistent—leaving a significant economic incentive for further illegal immigration."[78]

Walser, McNeill, and Zuckerman maintain that the solution to these problems is the implementation of both national and foreign policy. They believe America must continue to cooperate with nations to combat human smuggling and to open up foreign economies through free-market reforms, thus making emigration less attractive. To create more of a disincentive, the Heritage Foundation and others insist that the United States should tighten its border security, pursue and deport those who have entered the country illegally, and reject all amnesty proposals that simply give hope to illegal immigrants. "The dream of a better life via illegal migration is increasingly an illusion. Criminal organizations are increasingly adept at and entirely ruthless in exploiting the vulnerabilities of illegal immigrants,"[79] Walser, McNeill, and Zuckerman argue, asserting that weak border enforcement is dangerous for immigrants. They maintain that lax enforcement only encourages more immigrants to make the dangerous journey—especially across the US-Mexico border—and likely fall prey to traffickers. This, they claim, is worsening, not reducing, a humanitarian crisis along the border.

Looking Toward Reform

The United States has a patchwork of immigration laws and no agreed-upon policy to deal with the 11 million illegal immigrants who already live here or the thousands who attempt unlawful entry every day. As a result, politicians and pundits on both sides of the issue forecast tragedy. Human rights advocates maintain that no policy or regulation should put undocumented individuals in harm's way or deprive them of their dignity. Most citizens tend to support these protections; as Peter J. Duignan, a senior fellow of the Hoover Institution, wrote in 2003, "Americans are particularly opposed to illegal immigration, although not to undocumented aliens as individuals."[80] Despite Americans' humane outlook, reports of abuses at the border and within the detention system occur regularly. In addition, many illegal immigrants are victimized by human traffickers and other criminals who have little regard for human rights. There is no guarantee that immigration reform will resolve these problems, but Americans across the political spectrum agree that the government must do something to preserve the principles of the nation and the welfare of all people who want to share in them.

Source Notes

Introduction: Between Sovereign Rights and Human Rights

1. Quoted in Amy Bracken, "Immigrants, Legal Groups Allege Harsh Treatment at U.S. Border," Public Radio International, August 1, 2013. www.pri.org.
2. Bracken, "Immigrants, Legal Groups Allege Harsh Treatment at U.S. Border."
3. Quoted in Bracken, "Immigrants, Legal Groups Allege Harsh Treatment at U.S. Border."

Chapter I: Deciding What Rights Apply to Undocumented Immigrants

4. Charles Hirschman, "The Impact of Immigration on American Society: Looking Backward to the Future," Border Battles: The U.S. Immigration Debates, July 28, 2006. http://border battles.ssrc.org.
5. Quoted in John Dillin, "How Eisenhower Solved Illegal Border Crossings from Mexico," *Christian Science Monitor*, July 6, 2006. www.csmonitor.com.
6. Quoted in Terry Gross, "America's Forgotten History of Mexican-American 'Repatriation,'" *Fresh Air*, National Public Radio, September 10, 2015. www.npr.org.
7. *Slate*, "Do Noncitizens Have Constitutional Rights?," September 27, 2001. www.slate.com.
8. *Slate*, "Do Noncitizens Have Constitutional Rights?"
9. Erwin Chemerinsky, "Even Terrorism Suspects Have Rights," *Los Angeles Times*, May 11, 2010. www.latimes.com.
10. Phil Roe, "Illegal Immigration Is a Serious Threat to America's National Security," *Congress Blog*, Hill, April 26, 2012. www.thehill.com.
11. Peter B. Gemma, "Illegal Alien Crime and Violence by the Numbers: We're All Victims," Constitution Party. www.constitutionparty.com.

12. Donald Trump, "Presidential Campaign Announcement," C-SPAN, June 16, 2015. www.cspan.com.
13. Tanya Golash-Boza, "Human Rights or Civil Rights for Immigrants?," *ACSblog*, American Constitution Society, April 12, 2012. www.acslaw.org.
14. Golash-Boza, "Human Rights or Civil Rights for Immigrants?"
15. Quoted in Rick Scuteri, "U.N. Warns States on Illegal Immigrant Rights," Reuters, September 30, 2010. www.reuters .com.
16. Jack Goldsmith, "Should International Human Rights Law Trump US Domestic Law?," *Chicago Journal of International Law*, September 1, 2000, p. 339.
17. Jeremy Rabkin, "The Human Rights Agenda Versus National Sovereignty," Freedom House, 2016. www.freedomhouse.org.

Chapter 2: Harassment and Exploitation

18. Quoted in *The Takeaway*, "Americans Find Ways to Support Undocumented Immigrants," Public Radio International, March 12, 2012. www.pri.org.
19. American Civil Liberties Union, "Preliminary Analysis of HB 56 'Alabama Taxpayer and Citizen Protection Act,'" June 13, 2011. www.aclu.org.
20. Amanda Peterson Beadle, "Alabama's HB 56 Anti-Immigrant Law Takes Final Gasps," American Immigration Council, October 30, 2013. www.immigrationimpact.com.
21. Muzaffar Chishti and Faye Hipsman, "Alabama Settlement Marks Near End of a Chapter in State Immigration Enforcement Activism," Migration Policy Institute, November 14, 2013. www.migrationpolicy.org.
22. Human Rights Watch, "No Way to Live: Alabama's Immigrant Law," December 14, 2011. www.hrw.org.
23. *International Convention on the Elimination of All Forms of Racial Discrimination*, New York, United Nations Human Rights Office of the High Commissioner, January 4, 1969. www .ohchr.org.
24. Chris Good, "Arizona's Immigration Law Is Popular. Is Racial Profiling?," *Atlantic*, May 4, 2010. www.theatlantic.com.
25. American Civil Liberties Union, "Question of the Violation of Human Rights and Fundamental Freedoms in Any Part of the World," March 23, 2005. www.aclu.org.

26. Human Rights Watch, "No Way to Live."

27. Human Rights Watch, "No Way to Live."

28. Arturo Gonzalez, "Putting Limits on Day Laborers: Proliferating Local Ordinances Don't Address the Demand for Workers," Public Policy Institute of California, April 15, 2007. www.ppic.org.

29. Southern Poverty Law Center, "Injustice on Our Plates," November 7, 2010. www.splcenter.org.

30. Southern Poverty Law Center, "Alabama's Shame: HB 56 and the War on Immigrants," January 31, 2012. www.splcenter.org.

31. Human Rights Watch, "Cultivating Fear: The Vulnerability of Immigrant Farmworkers in the US to Sexual Violence and Sexual Harassment," May 15, 2012. www.hrw.org.

32. Quoted in Dave Jamieson, "Undocumented Worker Alleges Wage Theft, Ends Up in Deportation Proceedings," *Huffington Post*, July 9, 2013. www.huffingtonpost.com.

33. Quoted in Jamieson, "Undocumented Worker Alleges Wage Theft, Ends Up in Deportation Proceedings."

34. Human Rights Watch, "US: Sexual Violence, Harassment of Immigrant Farmworkers," *Huffington Post*, May 16, 2012. www.huffingtonpost.com.

Chapter 3: Detention and Deportation

35. Quoted in Human Rights Watch, "Jailing Refugees: Arbitrary Detention of Refugees in the US Who Fail to Adjust to Permanent Resident Status," December 29, 2009. www.hrw.org.

36. Human Rights Watch, "Jailing Refugees."

37. John F. Simanski, "Immigration Enforcement Actions: 2013," Department of Homeland Security, 2014. www.dhs.gov.

38. Quoted in AJ Vicens, "The Obama Administration's 2 Million Deportations, Explained," Mother Jones, April 4, 2014. www.motherjones.com.

39. Amnesty International, "Jailed Without Justice: Immigration Detention in the USA," March 25, 2009. www.amnestyusa.org.

40. Alexandra Cole, "Prisoners of Profit: Immigrants and Detention in Georgia," American Civil Liberties Union of Georgia, May 27, 2016. www.acluga.org.

41. Amnesty International, "Jailed Without Justice."

42. Cole, "Prisoners of Profit."

43. Azadeh N. Shahshahani, "Prisoners of Profit: Immigrants and Detention in Georgia," May 30, 2012. www.aclu.org.

44. Amnesty International, "Jailed Without Justice."

45. Elise Foley, "Complaint Alleges Sexual Abuse in Immigrant Detention Center," *Huffington Post*, October 2, 2014. www.huffingtonpost.com.

46. Amnesty International, "Jailed Without Justice."

47. Paul Pauker, "The Morality of Mass Deportation," *American Thinker*, August 24, 2015. www.americanthinker.com.

48. International Covenant on Civil and Political Rights, New York, United Nations Human Rights Office of the High Commissioner, March 23, 1976. www.ohchr.org.

49. Joanna Dreby, "How Today's Immigration Enforcement Policies Impact Children, Families, and Communities," Center for American Progress, August 2012. www.americanprogress.org.

50. Amnesty International, "Jailed Without Justice."

51. Dreby, "How Today's Immigration Enforcement Policies Impact Children, Families, and Communities."

52. Quoted in Richard Fausset, "Immigration: ACLU Alleges Rights Violations at Detention Centers," *Los Angeles Times*, May 16, 2012. www.latimes.com.

53. Denise Gilman, "Realizing Liberty: The Use of International Human Rights Law to Realign Immigration Detention in the United States," *Fordham International Law Journal*, February 2013, p. 248.

Chapter 4: Human Trafficking

54. Tiffany Williams, "Key Facts from 'The Dual Mandate: Immigration Enforcement and Human Trafficking,'" Institute for Policy Studies, January 10, 2013. www.ips-dc.org.

55. Williams, "Key Facts from 'The Dual Mandate.'"

56. Federation for American Immigration Reform, "Human Trafficking—Exploitation of Illegal Aliens," 2016. www.fairus.org.

57. Lisa Olsen, "Crackdown on Houston Sex Ring Freed 120 Women," *Houston (TX) Chronicle*, June 29, 2008. www.chron.com.

58. Quoted in Olsen, "Crackdown on Houston Sex Ring Freed 120 Women."

59. Legal Immigration for America executive director, "Illegal Immigration and Sex Trafficking," Legal Immigration for America, June 16, 2016. www.golifa.com.
60. Texas Department of Public Safety, "Assessing the Threat of Human Trafficking in Texas," April 2014. www.txdps.state.tx.us.
61. US Department of Homeland Security, "Blue Campaign." www.dhs.gov.
62. *Investor's Business Daily*, "For Human Traffickers, Obama's Border Policy Is a Bonanza," August 25, 2015. www.investors.com.
63. Joy Ngozi Ezeilo, "Report of the Special Rapporteur on Trafficking in Persons, Especially Women and Children," United Nations Human Rights Council, June 6, 2012. www.ohchr.org.
64. Federation for American Immigration Reform, "Human Trafficking—Exploitation of Illegal Aliens."

Chapter 5: Policies and Prevention Efforts

65. Jeh Johnson, "Remarks by Secretary of Homeland Security Jeh Charles Johnson on 'Immigration: Perception Versus Reality' at Rice University," Department of Homeland Security, June 8, 2015. www.dhs.gov.
66. Quoted in Ariane de Vogue, "Obama Administration Wants Supreme Court to Approve Its Immigration Plans," CNN, November 10, 2015. www.cnn.com.
67. Quoted in Nicholas Kristof, "Obama's Death Sentence for Young Refugees," *New York Times*, June 25, 2016. www.nytimes.com.
68. Quoted in Joseph Sorrentino, "How the U.S. 'Solved' the Central American Migrant Crisis," *In These Times*, May 12, 2015. www.inthesetimes.com.
69. Kristof, "Obama's Death Sentence for Young Refugees."
70. Quoted in Alan Gomez, "Raids Target Undocumented Immigrants in Georgia, North Carolina and Texas," *USA Today*, January 4, 2016. www.usatoday.com.
71. Human Rights Watch, "Statement to the US Commission on Civil Rights on Immigration Detention Facilities," March 2, 2015. www.hrw.org.
72. Human Rights Watch, "'You Don't Have Rights Here': US Border Screening and Returns of Central Americans to Risk of Serious Harm," October 16, 2014. www.hrw.com.

73. Quoted in Aileen B. Flores, "ACLU Claims Abusive Treatment by CBP Officers," *El Paso (TX) Times*, May 17, 2016. www .elpasotimes.com.

74. Quoted in US Customs and Border Protection, "CBP Addresses Humanitarian Challenges of Unaccompanied Child Migrants," July 21, 2014. www.cbp.gov.

75. Gary Gutting and Joseph Carens, "When Immigrants Lose Their Human Rights," *Opinionator* (blog), *New York Times*, November 25, 2014. www.opinionator.blogs.nytimes.com.

76. Amnesty International, *In Hostile Terrain: Human Rights Violations in Immigration Enforcement in the US Southwest*. New York: Amnesty International, 2012, p. 74.

77. Quoted in Fox News, "Border Patrol's Website Offers Advice on Eluding . . . Border Patrol," August 2, 2016. www.foxnews .com.

78. Ray Walser, Jena Baker McNeill, and Jessica Zuckerman, "The Human Tragedy of Illegal Immigration: Greater Efforts Needed to Combat Smuggling and Violence," Backgrounder #2568, Heritage Foundation, June 22, 2011. www.heritage .org.

79. Walser, McNeill, and Zuckerman, "The Human Tragedy of Illegal Immigration."

80. Peter J. Duignan, "Making and Remaking America: Immigration into the United States," Hoover Institution, September 15, 2003. www.hoover.org.

How To Get Involved

By getting involved, you can make a difference. Organizations that work with human rights and immigration often need volunteers for a variety of tasks ranging from letter writing to organizing events. Some organizations also sponsor internships for youth.

American Civil Liberties Union (ACLU)
125 Broad St., 18th Floor
New York, NY 10004
www.aclu.org

The ACLU is one of the nation's oldest civil rights watchdog groups. The websites of ACLU branches within each state inform young people on how to get involved with the organization. They also provide calendars of upcoming ACLU meetings and educational essays on issues affecting young people in their state and across the nation.

Amnesty International (USA Headquarters)
5 Penn Plaza, 16th Floor
New York, NY 10001
www.amnestyusa.org

Amnesty International is a global organization focused on protecting human rights. The organization has branches in various countries. Young people are encouraged to get involved with the organization's activities, which range from publishing newsletters and fact sheets to lobbying governments for change in their human rights behavior.

Human Rights Watch (HRW)
350 Fifth Ave., 34th Floor
New York, NY 10118
www.hrw.org

HRW is a nonprofit, nongovernmental organization of experts who perform fact-finding, reporting, and advocacy on behalf of those whose rights are in jeopardy. HRW lobbies governments for change and otherwise brings to light human rights violations around the globe. The organization provides internships in field offices in larger US cities and in major foreign cities.

National Network for Immigrant and Refugee Rights (NNIRR)

www.nnirr.org

Founded in 1986, the NNIRR concerns itself with the protection and expansion of immigrant rights regardless of immigration status. The organization offers workshops and downloads on immigrant issues. It also offers internships throughout the year in areas such as immigration policy, border justice, international migrant rights, and immigration.

Southern Poverty Law Center (SPLC)

400 Washington Ave.
Montgomery, AL 36104
www.splcenter.org

The SPLC is a network of legal experts who take on clients facing discrimination or other civil rights abuses. The SPLC has worked to educate the public, launch lawsuits, and create awareness about immigrant rights. The organization has no youth staff positions, but in 2002 it launched a Teaching Tolerance campaign to promote discussions of social boundaries in schools.

Youth for Human Rights International (YHRI)

1920 Hillhurst Ave. #416
Los Angeles, CA 90027
www.youthforhumanrights.org

YHRI is a global nongovernmental organization that teaches young people about the Universal Declaration of Human Rights and issues relating to the declaration's application and enforcement. The group provides educational materials and sponsors workshops to engage new members. YHRI assists young people in creating human rights groups in their schools or communities.

For Further Research

Books

Aviva Chomsky, *Undocumented: How Immigration Became Illegal*. Boston: Beacon, 2014.

Stephen Currie, *Undocumented Immigrant Youth.* San Diego, CA: ReferencePoint, 2017.

Tanya Maria Golash-Boza, *Immigration Nation: Raids, Detentions, and Deportations in Post-9/11 America*. New York: Routledge, 2012.

David M. Haugen, *What Should Be Done About Illegal Immigration?* San Diego, CA: ReferencePoint, 2017.

Marie Friedmann Marquardt et al., *Living "Illegal": The Human Face of Unauthorized Immigration*. New York: New Press, 2013.

Walter Nicholls, *The DREAMers: How the Undocumented Youth Movement Transformed the Immigrant Rights Debate*. Stanford, CA: Stanford University Press, 2013.

Terry Sterling, *Illegal: Life and Death in Arizona's Immigration War Zone*. Guilford, CT: Lyons, 2010.

Kim Voss and Irene Bloemraad, eds., *Rallying for Immigrant Rights: The Fight for Inclusion in 21st Century America*. Berkeley: University of California Press, 2011.

Internet Sources

American Immigration Council, "Removal Without Recourse: The Growth of Summary Deportations from the United States," April 28, 2014. http://immigrationpolicy.org/just-facts/removal-with out-recourse-growth-summary-deportations-united-states.

Arian Campo-Flores, "Arizona's Immigration Law and Racial Profiling," *Newsweek*, April 26, 2010. www.newsweek.com/arizo nas-immigration-law-and-racial-profiling-70683.

Walter Ewing, "The U.S. Deportation System's Human Toll," American Immigration Council, May 27, 2014. http://immigrationim pact.com/2014/05/27/the-u-s-deportation-systems-human-toll.

Howard W. Foster, "Why More Immigration Is Bad for America," *The Buzz* (blog), *National Interest*, September 5, 2014. http:// nationalinterest.org/blog/the-buzz/why-more-immigration-bad -america-11210.

Carrie Kuehl, "The Humanity Behind Illegal Immigration," *Human Rights* (blog), *Albany (NY) Times Union*, April 28, 2014. http:// blog.timesunion.com/humanrights/the-humanity-behind-illegal -immigration/527.

Michael Oleaga, "Millennials on Immigration: Government Should Not Deport All Immigrants from US," *Latin Post*, December 7, 2015. www.latinpost.com/articles/99961/20151207/millennials -on-immigration-government-should-not-deport-all-immigrants -from-us.htm.

Elizabeth Perez, "Illegal Immigration & Human Trafficking," *Patriot Statesman*, June 11, 2011. http://patriotstatesman.com /2011/06/illegal-immigration-human-trafficking.

Jessica M. Vaughan, "Deportation Numbers Unwrapped," backgrounder, Center for Immigration Studies, 2013. http://cis.org /ICE-Illegal-Immigrant-Deportations.

Danny Vinik, "How Much Would It Cost to Deport All Undocumented Immigrants?," *New Republic*, July 8, 2014. https://ne wrepublic.com/article/118602/deporting-all-undocumented -immigrants-would-cost-billions-immigration.

Index